# Paper Cuts:
# My Life in Chicago's Volatile LGBTQ Press

## Rick Karlin

Rattling Good Yarns Press
33490 Date Palm Drive 3065
Cathedral City CA 92235
USA
www.rattlinggoodyarns.com

Cover Design: Ian Henzel, LeatherLeaf Marketing & Design

Library of Congress Control Number: 2019952894
ISBN: 978-1-7341464-1-7


First Edition

For my husband Gregg and my son Adam

# FOREWORD

\* \* \*

When I received the manuscript for this book, the first thing that jumped out at me was the word "volatile." I laughed. It's the perfect word to describe working for any newspaper. In the Cambridge Dictionary, the definition of the word "volatile" reads: "Likely to change suddenly and unexpectedly, or suddenly violent or angry." Another good word to describe it would be "toxic," of which the definition is: "Poisonous, or relating to poisonous substances." Both words accurately describe my three decades of working for the LGBTQ press. However, I learned early on how to survive – ignore everyone else and stay focused. You also need a thick skin, the hide of a rhinoceros.

Writing for a newspaper is setting yourself up as a target. I've been professionally stabbed in the back so often, that I'm beginning to look like a hedgehog. I don't mind, I quite like hedgehogs. Insults, character assassinations, etc. only work if the recipient plays the role of victim and either collapses under the weight of it all or takes the bait and fights back. I do neither. I don't even notice. I was once on a panel at the Harold Washington Library with three other notables in the Chicago gay community. After it was over, a woman approached me from the audience and said, "I'm sorry you had to go through that." "Go through what?" I asked. "Two of those people on the panel were very nasty to you." She named them. I won't but you know who they are. I hadn't even noticed. I was too busy answering questions from the audience.

When I was working for the LGBTQ press, I gave myself this brief – to educate and entertain the readers, bring advertisers to the paper, and cover every aspect of the community. Instead of engaging in time-consuming ugly brawls with competitors, I put my energy into writing articles to the best of my ability. In short, I ignored everybody else. If I want somebody else's input, I'll ask for it. But don't hold your breath. It's not happening.

So yes, "volatile" is a perfect word.

Rick Karlin and I began working for the LGBTQ press around the same time. I was in Britain writing columns and feature articles for *Capital Gay*, *Gay Times*, and the *Pink Paper*. Karlin was in Chicago, that great metropolis along the shores of Lake Michigan. I arrived in the Windy City in 1991 and began writing for Tracy Baim's *Outlines* soon after that. I know it's a sexist generalization, but I prefer working for women. Not because they're warm and cuddly and have maternal instincts ... no, no, no. I prefer working for women because when you screw up, they'll tell you upfront. No gossiping behind your back, no nudging you out. You know where you stand. I've always had a good working relationship with Ms. Baim. I have nothing but admiration for everything she has achieved. After *Outlines*, *Nightspots,* and *Windy City Times*, I moved to *Chicago Free Press*, then *Gay Chicago* and *ChicagoPride.com*. Like most writers in the LGBTQ press in Chicago, I was passed around like a joint at a Grateful Dead concert. But that's my story.

*Paper Cuts: My Life in Chicago's Volatile LGBTQ Press* is the story of Rick Karlin's life writing for Chicago's newspapers, balancing that with his family life outside of it. Joining the staff at *GayLife* in 1978 gave Karlin a front-row seat at some of the momentous events in post-Stonewall LGBTQ history. From the privileged vantage point of a newspaper office, he watched the rise and fall of disco, the AIDS crisis, same sex marriage, bars opening and closing, and LGBTQ newspapers coming and going. Like gossip columnists, Hedda Hopper and Louella Parsons, Karlin knew the dirt going on behind the scenes. He wasn't frightened to publish it in his gossip column either, sometimes to his detriment.

When I embark on history research for my books and articles, I look back at LGBTQ newspapers and go to the gossip column first. I'm interested in the minutiae of the goings on. Gossip columns about the rich and famous don't interest me. I'd rather read that a certain local drag queen is working three jobs to save enough money to move to New York. It tells us about the everyday lives of LGBTQ's in Chicago. Not what Boy George, Elton John, or Ellen Degeneres are up to. But how regular people like us lived. How we lived, loved, and struggled to survive in a hostile world.

As Karlin alludes to in his book, working for a newspaper can be a lonely business. It can also be a thankless task. I've never been enamored with being a celebrity myself. Though I have to say that getting your name and face in the paper every week does open doors for you. Like Karlin, I've been to some of the most select fundraisers, at which I take pictures, ask questions, and leave. I don't care to schmooze, hit the buffet, or suck up.

As a reporter for the LGBTQ press, I never considered myself to be a part of the gay community. I had my own private life, and I "covered" the LGBTQ community. To the reader it looked like I was in the middle of it all. Some readers could be forgiven for thinking that I was a "mover and shaker," out there with all the local celebrities and A gays. That's a laugh, not once was I ever invited to their BBQ's or social events at their homes. They just wanted me to put them in the paper. They didn't want me as a friend. I knew that. Not quite true, now I come to think about it. Local businessman and bar/baths owner, Chuck Renslow, once invited me for Thanksgiving dinner and to join his Freemason's Lodge. I didn't go to dinner as it would be a conflict of interest. And I'd rather get my eyeballs pierced than join the Freemason's. But I very much appreciated the offer, though. Chuck was a true gentleman.

As I mostly stayed clear of the "newspaper wars," I was fascinated by *Paper Cuts* because it documents the "goings-on" behind the scenes of the LGBTQ press in Chicago. Not something you usually read about. When I was the Associate Editor of *Windy City Times* and Managing Editor of *Nightspots* magazine, I never had time to think about what the other papers were up to. Now I know. *Paper Cuts* tells the story of a man wrestling with fatherhood while trying to carve out an identity for himself as a gay man in the 1970s. Like all of our lives, Karlin had his highs and lows.

So why do we do it? Why do we work in a toxic environment for little pay? The rough and tumble of a newspaper office is not pretty. Tensions run high, exhaustion is an enemy, the next step is drugs and alcohol. I'm no stranger to those two. Longevity in the gay press is about picking your battles and knowing when to shut up. To work for the gay press is to be an activist. In my case, I never joined ACT UP protests, Queer Nation stunts, etc. As a reporter, I had to remain impartial. Activism, for me, was covering the story. Karlin wasn't a waving the banner type of activist either. Instead, he was an editor, gossip columnist, food writer and also a playwright. His activism served the LGBTQ community in raising thousands of dollars for various charities. Nobody organizes fundraisers like Rick Karlin. It's a gift. A gift of stubbornness and tenacity.

Karlin recently became the Director of Communications for the Chicago LGBTQ Hall of Fame. It seems so fitting that his memoir is framed within the bios of those Chicago news folks inducted. Of course, the bios are frozen in time like Andy Warhol's screen prints of Marilyn Monroe, Elizabeth Taylor, Mick Jagger, and Elvis Presley. The Hall of Fame bios are never updated, they stand like stone monuments, a sort of PressHenge.

Scratch the veneer of what Karlin calls his "so-called celebrity" and you will find a man of conviction, morals, and a keen sense of community. In short, Rick Karlin is a jewel in the crown of Chicago's LGBTQ press. In 1978 he dived into a polluted pool and, holding his nose, swam in it for decades. And Chicago is all the better for it.

— St Sukie de la Croix, Palm Springs, CA 2019

# INTRODUCTION

## ✳ ✳ ✳

When I was 25 years old, I was asked a question that would change my life, "Do you think you could do it?"

Perhaps I should back up a bit. It was 1978 and the media was full of articles about, and coverage of "Gay Lib." It was the era when, "The love that dare not speak its name," refused to be silent any longer. Even with all that media coverage, you didn't hear much about guys like me; a newly out gay man with a young son.

My coming out story is similar to so many others, stories that have been told a thousand times. The only difference was I had a child, and I wasn't going to give up on being a father. It was the one thing that I knew I could do right. After I came out, I found a support group for other gays and lesbians with children. Since I worked downtown, I was asked to drop off the classified ad about the group's meetings at *GayLife* newspaper each week. One day I mentioned to *GayLife* staff that I missed some of the cooking columns they had run. I asked if they planned to reinstate the column at any time in the future. They informed me that the writer had moved out of town and offered to let me write it, asking that loaded question, "Do you think you could do it?"

I was shocked to hear myself say that I would try. I'd previously never risen to that kind of challenge. Still, I don't think I'd ever been given that kind of opportunity before. That simple answer led me on an incredible journey. It allowed me to meet people I would have never had the chance to meet. It also allowed me to experience a broader spectrum of life than I would have thought possible.

More than 40 years later, that unsure 25-year-old became one of the elders of Chicago's LGBTQ media. As papers folded, I moved on to others, expanded the focus of my writing, and adapted to changes in the business. Am I the best writer that Chicago LGBTQ press has seen? Not by far. Am I the most prolific writer? No, many others who hold that title. Yet, somehow, not only did I manage to survive, I thrived.

In his extensive history of the LGBTQ press, *Unspeakable: The Rise of the Gay and Lesbian Press in America* Rodger Streitmatter states, "The most important contribution lesbian and gay journalism has made – and will continue to make ... reading gay publications has served as a first tenuous step for men and women embarking on the very personal and often profoundly difficult journey toward acknowledging their homosexuality to themselves and the world around them."

That proved especially true for me. The LGBTQ press provided the opportunity for me to take those first tenuous steps, made easier because I now knew that I was not alone. Those steps, like Dorothy on the Yellow Brick Road, led me to experiences I otherwise never would have encountered.

*Paper Cuts* is my recollection of writing for Chicago's LGBTQ press for more than four decades. I don't purport to be historically objective. Some timelines may have gotten a little jumbled – after all, I did live through the '70s and '80s. But I hope to give an accurate report of my journey, ranging from the time when I handed in "hard copy," to electronically uploading my files, to syncing computers across the country – and always facing a deadline.

# CHAPTER 1

All my life, I felt ashamed about the way I looked, about the way I walked, about the way I did ... everything. My father constantly taunted me about my weight and how useless I was. I now realize that my parents were overwhelmed with raising five kids. How else to explain that they never noticed I was so near-sighted as to be nearly blind? It wasn't until I was 13 years old and failed an eye-test at school that they bothered to take me to an eye doctor. Of course, I was terrible at sports – Hello! I couldn't see the ball. I couldn't handle tools or fix things – it turns out I'm dyslexic as well! As far as my father was concerned, I was a useless sissy.

I was in kindergarten when I realized I was not like other boys. I remember watching a man jumping on a trampoline on television. With every bounce, an article of clothing flew off. When his pants came off, I felt a tingle in my groin. Somehow, even then, I knew that I shouldn't feel that excitement. In 1969 I read the bestselling *Everything You Always Wanted to Know About Sex: But Were Afraid to Ask* by Dr. David Reuben. The dismal, and inaccurate, description of gay life only reinforced my fear and self-loathing. I was 11 years old when I first acted upon my desires. I "fooled around" with Stevie, a distant cousin a few years older than I was. It ended disastrously. Basically, Stevie let me fondle him until he got an erection. Then he panicked and pushed me away. I, of course, thought that I did it wrong. Another thing I wasn't good at!

A couple of days later, my mother called me into her bedroom. I knew I was in trouble. Stevie must have told on me. My mother had tears in her eyes as she explained that Stevie had died that night. She knew we were close – the two oldest boys in the family – and she knew I'd be upset by the news, but I don't think even she was ready for my reaction. I ran into my bedroom and slammed the door. I literally crawled into my closet and asked God to forgive me. I was sure it was my fault. It wasn't until years later I found out he was drinking beer with friends and had passed out and drowned in his own vomit.

Of course, there were other times growing up when boys made overtures, as boys, gay or straight, often do when they're raging with hormones. I'd pretend I didn't know what they meant. I had one sexual experience in high school with a classmate. Another time I was fondled by a neighborhood barber. Each time I was wracked with guilt. I was so sure they would die as Stevie had, that I never followed through on the experience, kicking myself later for my cowardice.

In my freshman year of college, I met a beautiful Chinese-American woman in an art class. We went on a few dates, and she said she loved me. Although I was not sexually attracted to her, I thought, as many people of that time did, that the love of a good woman would help curb my desires. Soon after we married, I realized I still had those feelings and that the marriage wasn't going to help. I decided to tell her about my feelings and ask for a divorce. The day when I finally worked up the courage to talk to her, she told me she was pregnant.

Then I thought that maybe being a father would make the attraction to men go away. As much as I loved my son Adam when he was born, it didn't. But that was all right, as I was so in love with my son and being a father that I thought nothing else mattered. About six months after my son was born, I was at a downtown subway stop waiting for the train after working my night shift at a bank. When the train arrived shortly after midnight, I found myself sitting across from a very handsome man. He had dirty blond hair that feathered away from his head with bangs that swept over his dark brows. He was holding a giant stuffed toy giraffe. He smiled and winked. I turned around to see who was behind me. Since it was after midnight, we were the only two people in the train car. When I turned back, he laughed and pointed to me and said, "You're so cute."

I looked down and mumbled something. He crossed the aisle and sat next to me, putting the giraffe on the other side of him. I asked about the stuffed animal, and he told me it was for a friend who just had a baby. As we talked, he occasionally stroked my arm or leg. I was enchanted. The train pulled into a station; he rose and headed for the car door. He turned and smiled and said, "I hope I see you again."

Even though it wasn't my stop, I exited with him and followed him up the stairs. He turned and smiled and said, "Well, it took you long enough. I've been flirting with you since Division Street. He told me his name was Chris Carlson and asked if I had a place nearby. Not only was I miles from my house, but my wife and son were also at home. When I explained that I didn't have a place we could go to, he said that he was supposed to meet friends anyway. After an awkward silence, he asked if we could meet up that weekend. As luck would have it, my wife was taking the baby to Florida to see her sister. I didn't have any vacation time, so I couldn't go with her. Chris and I could meet, but I didn't tell him about my wife.

I almost didn't go through with our meeting, but on that Saturday, I found myself standing on the pre-determined spot, both hoping and dreading that he would show up. Ten minutes after our appointed time, I was just about to leave when he came around the corner. I had never been so happy to see anyone before. Within five minutes, I admitted my wife was away, and we went back to my apartment and made love for hours. He was much more experienced than I was and was a tender and patient lover. I finally knew what I had been missing from my life; passion. I had never felt so alive – or so guilty.

As he later revealed, Chris was also married. His wife Judy had just come home from the hospital with the baby the night we met – hence the stuffed giraffe. For about three months we carried on a clandestine love affair. We both worked the four to midnight shift downtown. Like most urban centers at the time, Chicago's "Loop" was deserted at night. There were few places open, we opted for Ron Briskman's Hideout, a restaurant in the lower level of an office building. It was a bustling spot during the day serving lunch to office and department store workers. In the evening, it catered to a mostly gay clientele. We would both take long dinner breaks, even if it meant we had to work later. During our trysts, we'd hold hands and make out. Our waiter Vinny, the first "screaming queen" I had ever met, thought we were the most romantic thing. Vinny became a friend and let us use his place on Saturday afternoons when our wives thought we were running errands. I was in love for the first time in my life.

After a few months, my guilt and the fact that I knew I would never be happy with my wife, led me to come out to her. It was one of the most painful things I ever did. A few days afterward, I told Chris what I'd done. The next day, he broke the news to me that the hotel chain he worked for was transferring him to Denver. By the end of the month, he was gone.

My wife and I decided to remain together until the baby was old enough to go into daycare. Now we were living like roommates and barely spoke to each other. After Chris left, I still went to the Hideout for dinner and found a copy of *GayLife,* the city's gay newspaper. Other than my waiter friend Vinny, I didn't know any gay people and sank into a deep depression. *GayLife* became my lifeline. It gave me a sense of belonging to a community. Most of the events I read about in *GayLife* took place in bars and clubs. I had never gone to bars, either when I was single or married. It just wasn't what my friends did – I guess we were nerds. The idea of going to a gay bar hadn't entered my mind. In fact, the thought of entering a gay bar terrified me.

I knew there was such a thing as a gay bar. As a child, there was one in our neighborhood. My parents had always warned us to stay away from it. Of course, that made me even more curious. While riding my bike, I would take a surreptitious look in the small windows that flanked the front door. They were covered by a heavy curtain. Not that I would have seen much anyway, as it was during the day that I rode past it.

One night I noticed an ad for a bar called the 21 Club, on Irving Park Rd., just a few blocks from where my wife and I lived on the city's near Northwest side. That evening my loneliness got the better of me, and I decided to check it out. I got out of work at midnight, so it was about one in the morning when I approached the bar's entrance. I looked both ways on the street to make sure no-one I knew was around, then stepped into the recessed vestibule and grabbed the door handle. Like many gay bars at the time, you had to be buzzed in. When I pulled on the handle, the door didn't open; instead, I propelled myself forward, bumping the door with my head. I heard a buzz, so I walked in. The bar ran the length of the room. The men sitting at it all turned and looked at me. I took a seat, ordered a rum and Coke, and looked around. It all seemed so ordinary! I had honestly expected it to look like an opium den from the movie, *Thoroughly Modern Millie*. But instead, it was just a group of working-class men sitting at a bar, drinking beer, and having quiet conversations. Everyone was quite friendly, and I continued to stop by for a drink every night.

I loved hearing the older gay men – they must have been at least 40! – tell stories about the old days. I learned a lot about the gay culture at that bar. Being one of only three gay bars on Chicago's northwest side, it served as a meeting place for all sorts of people. Queens, toughs, "rough trade" and the occasional drag queen or Leatherman. There were no women in the bar, ever!

And yet, I didn't quite fit in the 21 Club either. When they found out I had a two-year-old son, they looked at me as if I were from another planet. More than once I was asked if I was sure I was gay.

A year later, my wife and I separated. She and her recently divorced sister shared an apartment together in the suburbs, and Adam went to a nursery school while my wife was at work. I kept our small city apartment, which suddenly seemed spacious, as I had no furniture. I didn't tell my family or friends why we separated, but since we'd married so young, they weren't surprised.

One week, soon after we separated, there was an ad in the classified section of *GayLife* for a gay parents' rap group. It had been placed by a lesbian mother of two, who bravely listed her phone number as a contact. I called it immediately. Kathy Ramos, the woman who placed the ad, and I hit it off and talked on the phone several times before the first meeting. After a few weeks, enough people had responded, so Kathy invited everyone over to her apartment. As soon as I walked in, I felt that I had found my place in the community. These were gay people who, like me, were glad to be mothers and fathers. Some were still married, some divorced, and many were still in the closet, as was I.

The classified ads in *GayLife* provided other contacts that changed my life. One was positive; I saw an advertisement about organizing a fundraiser for WTTW, the local PBS station. It had recently aired *The Word is Out*, one of the first documentaries to present gay people in a positive light. I called the number and spoke to the organizer, Chris Clason, and went to a few meetings. I don't remember much about what we did, or how often we met, but it must have done some good.

# Chris Clason

For several years in the 1970s and 1980s, Chris Clason was a talented, entertaining figure as a singer-comic on local stages. He was also an Actors Equity member and worked onstage and backstage in community theater, children's theater, and professional dinner theater as well as modeling. He had several other jobs in restaurants, catering, even the U.S. Environmental Protection Agency.

But Clason is best remembered as the chief founder of Test Positive Aware Network (TPAN), which in his nonbureaucratic, visionary, and proactive way he established in 1987 on the basis of responses to an ad he had placed in *Gay Chicago*. He then served as its first executive director for two years.

TPAN was the first support network organized to reach out to all people who have tested positive for HIV, providing a combination of information and moral support. After his TPAN tenure, Clason moved to Howard Brown Memorial Clinic (now Health Center), where he served as education manager for nine months.

Clason was also a three-year member of the WTTW community advisory board and a member of city and state AIDS advisory councils. He organized *The Word Is Thanks*, a fundraiser in response to WTTW's presentation of the historical documentary *Word Is Out*.

Born in 1953 in Detroit, Clason graduated from Kimball High School in Royal Oak, Michigan, and completed two years as a theater major at Eastern Michigan University before moving to Chicago in 1972. In March 1990, in declining health, he moved to his parents' home in Oklahoma City. In Oklahoma, Chris sang in a gay chorus, took part in a bowling league, and helped plan the yearly gay and lesbian parade. He was also a speaker for the Regional AIDS Interfaith Network in Oklahoma City, where he died at age 38 in 1991 from complications of HIV infection.

Looking back in 1990 on his activist career during an interview with Bob Hultz, he characteristically spoke in favor of trying to maintain perspective as well as optimism: "I think our best focus for [TPAN] is to listen to the membership, to hear what people say. Look and see what draws people in, what satisfies them and provide that. . . . When everything about your life is attached to HIV and AIDS, it's like wearing yellow sunglasses all the time. Your world starts to get colored. But there are other colors in the rainbow. . . .

"Death and dying issues are major issues; we have all had to deal with the death of more friends and acquaintances than any of our parents. My parents are in their late 70s but they have not been exposed to the kind of death that I've been exposed to. . . . It will not be the same for generations after us. . . . It will be better and it will be worse. Just try to maintain the flexibility to handle whatever is coming up. I think death and dying is an important issue, but I think health and living is a very important issue; both deserve equal focus, if not a little extra on health and living issues."

Source: The Chicago LGBT Hall of Fame website at
glhalloffame.org
Clason was inducted in 2004, deceased 1991

Another classified ad drew my attention a few years later. I was paying my ex-wife more than a quarter of my salary in child support. I didn't have a problem with that – I knew she needed it to raise Adam – but the economic impact on me made my life difficult. My job as a pediatric therapist didn't pay well. Looking at the classifieds in *GayLife*, I saw an ad for part-time work, as an assistant to a contractor. I'd never done manual labor before, but I figured I could manage it if the guy was willing to teach me. I called the number and spoke to the man who placed the ad. He asked a lot of questions about my age and what I looked like. I figured out quickly that he wanted handsome young men, and I knew that I didn't qualify, so I started to end the conversation. Then he said that he'd meet with me, take me to his shop and see what I could do. As much as I wanted and needed that job, something didn't feel right. When he asked where I lived, I just told him the neighborhood. He offered to pick me up, so I told him I lived at home with my parents and asked him if we could meet elsewhere. He said he sometimes hung out at a neighborhood tavern on Elston Avenue, not too far from my apartment, and suggested a nearby intersection.

On the day of the appointment, I wore a pair of skimpy cut-off jean shorts and a tight T-shirt. I took a look in the mirror before I walked out the door. I was only a couple of years older than the 18-22 age range he'd noted in the ad. There was no way I was going to be thin or pretty, which I knew he expected. I decided not to show up. I hadn't given him my number, so he couldn't call me. It wasn't until a few months later that I realized how lucky I was. I am pretty confident that the contractor who wanted to meet me was the serial killer John Wayne Gacy. He often ran ads in *GayLife* looking for construction assistants, and he was known to frequent a bar close to where he asked me to meet him.

It was the ad for the parents' group in *GayLife* that most changed my life. I had become co-leader of the group and was responsible for submitting the group's classified ad in the paper each week. The ads were free but had to be mailed to or dropped off at the newspaper's downtown office. I expected the offices of *GayLife* to look like a scene from the movie, *The Front Page*. Instead, I found a dreary looking office and was greeted by a woman who looked like a heavier version of Janis Joplin. She stopped her furious typing long enough to take the 3"x5" card with the parents' group information and drop it into a wire basket with dozens of others.

That scene repeated itself every week for a few months. Eventually the woman was joined at a neighboring desk by a thin man with an enormous mustache. As the months went by, I worked up the courage to speak to them. I soon learned their names were Sarah Craig and Steve Kulieke, the editors of the newspaper. One day I mentioned to them that I enjoyed the cooking columns they'd run. Sarah said that the writer of that column had left town and asked me if I would like to take it over. I was a product of the Chicago Public School system and had never written anything more than a few essays in English class. Could I write? I didn't know. Since I didn't know what else to say, I told them I'd try and would bring them a column soon.

The cooking part didn't faze me; I've been interested in cooking since I was a child. When my son was born, I dropped out of college. I then managed to talk my way into a job at one of the city's most popular restaurants, where I worked my way up from line cook to sous chef within a year. Riding the subway home, the evening after the offer from *GayLife*, I took out a notepad and began to list possible topics for a column.

It was mid-summer; perhaps an article on picnic food would be appropriate. I jotted down some ideas and, when I got home, I pulled out my manual typewriter and typed up the recipes. I realized that I needed more than just a list of recipes. I added some ideas about how to make a picnic special by using real plates purchased from thrift stores and then throwing them away at the end of the picnic. I tried to work in some humor, hoping that maybe Steve and Sarah would enjoy it enough to run the column.

Then, I decided that column was too frivolous, so I wrote a second one on easy-to-prepare party food. The idea was that the host shouldn't spend the entire night in the kitchen. I titled it, "Out of the Kitchen and Into the Party." A play on the phrase "Out of the closet and into the streets" that was chanted at Gay Pride marches. For both columns, I used recipes that I had in my collection.

I returned the next day with the columns. As I handed them to Sarah, I was so nervous that my hand was shaking. I stood in front of her waiting for a response. It never occurred to me that she might have something more important to do. Seeing me standing there, she read the column and started laughing. She handed it over to Steve who also chuckled a few times.

"Thanks, we'll run it," was all he said.

Sarah added, "Deadlines are Monday. What do you want to call it?"

Celebrity TV chef Graham Kerr was known as "The Galloping Gourmet" at the time, so I offered, "The Gay Gourmet." On June 22, 1979, *GayLife* ran my first Gay Gourmet column. The next issue was for Independence Day, so they ran the picnic column.

# CHAPTER 2

There was never any talk of payment, and I honestly didn't expect any, I was thrilled to be a part of it all. Now, with my column running in the paper, I felt an even greater sense of belonging to a community. At that time, I handed in hard copy, typewritten pages that Sarah or Steve would edit. Those pages would be sent to the typesetter, before going to the art department for layout and paste-up. Eventually, Sarah, Steve and I, became friendly and socialized from time to time. I soon found myself in the inner circle that included the newspaper's art director, Lola Prunehill. Lola was a tall woman with a cackle of a laugh that could fill a room. I was so naïve that I didn't realize until years later that Lola was transgender. Even though her baritone and large hands should have been a tip-off.

Every year I would have a tree-trimming party. But, since I was so broke, I would provide art supplies and have all of the people attending make ornaments for my tree. Sarah Craig made a beautiful paper chicken that adorned my tree until it finally disintegrated. Ironically, the ornament outlived Sarah, who died in 1994 of a brain aneurysm.

I will remember Sarah for the smile on her cherubic face and how she was always willing to stop whatever-she-was-doing to chat when I dropped off my columns. Steve was usually brusque but, when not occupied, just as friendly.

I eventually met some of the other staff members, including Grant Ford, the newspaper's publisher, an avuncular man who was always calm and peaceful.

# Grant Ford

Grant Lynn Ford, 72, a former Assemblies of God minister who became an LGBT press pioneer and a dynamic Metropolitan Community Church pastor in the Chicago area and in Florida, where he now lives. He was founding publisher of *GayLife* in 1975 and ran for election as 44th Ward alderman in 1978.

Grant Lynn Ford was the founding publisher of the weekly (at first, fortnightly) *GayLife*, the city's first regularly scheduled community-based newspaper, which began in 1975. The paper eventually was distributed in several Midwestern cities. For several years *GayLife* also operated a telephone news line for late-breaking news and developing events.

Through *GayLife*, Ford was a founding member of the Gay and Lesbian Coalition of Metropolitan Chicago and of the Metropolitan Business Association. He was also a member of such organizations as Integrity/Chicago (an Episcopal LGBT group), Mattachine Midwest, and Together, an organization representing all alternative lifestyles.

In the late 1970s, Ford, along with community leader Chuck Renslow, sponsored Orange Balls I and II. These were Chicago benefits to raise funds to combat the Anita Bryant–backed anti-gay referendum in Dade County, Florida. Many community groups joined in a large demonstration during the singer's appearance at Chicago's Medinah Temple.

In 1978, Ford took a leave of absence from *GayLife* to run for 44th Ward alderman as an independent Democrat. He was one of the candidates endorsed by the Independent Voters of Illinois. When asked, "As a gay candidate, what will be your main concerns for Chicago?" he responded, "Garbage pickup, snow removal, and street repair. I'm running for City Council, just like everyone else." Gay rights were indeed an issue, but Ford made it clear he was not a one-issue candidate. Unfortunately, because of financial problems that arose during his absence from *GayLife*, Ford was forced to withdraw from the race weeks before the election to deal with them. Chuck Renslow bailed out the newspaper and assumed ownership.

A year later, Ford became pastor of Holy Covenant Metropolitan Community Church in Hinsdale, where he served until 1986. From 1981 to1986, he was abbot of the Poor Servants of Jesus, described as an ecumenical servite order. Ford served in consulting or supervising roles with MCC churches in Chicago and Evanston and was the founding pastor of Church of the Resurrection MCC in Chicago's Hyde Park neighborhood. During that time, he was also interim pastor of St. Paul's Lutheran Church in the Wicker Park neighborhood. In 1986, Ford became pastor of Florida's MCC Fort Lauderdale, which became Sunshine Cathedral and went on to become the MCC denomination's largest congregation. He ultimately served as dean of the cathedral until 2010.

Ford's compassion and community spirit were instrumental in the political, social, and spiritual development and visibility of Chicago's LGBT communities during the 1970s and 1980s.

Source: The Chicago LGBT Hall of Fame website at
glhalloffame.org
Ford was inducted in 2011, deceased 2019

# CHAPTER 3

B ecause of my column, I was invited to club openings, shows, and events. I was socializing with people I had only read about in *GayLife* – names I recognized from my first tenuous steps out of the closet a short time ago. With that kind of recognition and the confidence I gained from helping Kathy Ramos run the Gay Parents' Rap Group, I became more comfortable with who I was. I felt better about what I had to offer the world. I went back to college and got my bachelor's degree in education with a minor in therapeutic play. I landed a job at the University of Chicago Children's Hospital as a Child Life Therapist. I also came out to my immediate family and friends and was shocked that few of them were surprised. My mother, in fact, said that she always suspected. But she also asked me not to say anything to our extended family and neighbors.

When I told my mother that I was disappointed in her reaction, she responded, "It took you 25 years to come out, don't expect me to do it overnight." In later years, my mother, sisters, and surprisingly, my father, would all be incredibly supportive. It seemed that when I came out, all of his expectations of me changed.

Writing the column also helped stimulate other creative juices. I reconnected with an old high school friend when I discovered she and her husband lived in the building next door. They were developing a cabaret act of sorts, performing songs they had written. After seeing them perform one of their songs, *Saturday Night is the Loneliest Night*, at a nightclub, I went home and dreamt of a musical based on their songs. The next morning, I wrote down what I could remember, and we made plans to turn their songs into a musical based on my concept. My friends ended up moving out of town and that plan never came to fruition, but I kept the script. It would prove pivotal in a short time.

Since I only dropped off my column, I wasn't privy to the behind the scenes workings of the newspaper. When the office moved from a downtown building to 409 N. Franklin, far from where I worked, I started mailing in my column and didn't see much of the *GayLife* staff. In the fall of 1979, I noticed that Sarah wasn't listed in the masthead any longer. A week or so later when I picked up the next issue of the paper, there was an insert, a new lesbian newspaper, *Blazing Star*. Sarah Craig was listed as its editor.

It was a time when new technology, desktop computers, word processors, and smaller printing presses made publishing and editing newspapers for niche markets more feasible. The number of gay publications continued to grow at a rapid pace. In his book *Unspeakable*, Rodger Streitmatter notes that 600 gay and lesbian publications existed in the United States in 1980.

*Blazing Star* didn't last long. After a few issues, it didn't appear in *GayLife* or anywhere, and Sarah's name was gone from the *GayLife* masthead. In January of 1980, *GayLife* issued a tri-state off-shoot serving Ohio, Indiana, and Kentucky. The Chicago newspaper was in a new tabloid format, with Judy MacLean listed as editor. Now both Steve and Sarah were out. I kept mailing in my columns, addressing them simply to "Editor." By the February 1st, 1980 issue Steve and Sarah were back as co-editors, MacLean was listed as editor, beneath them. An odd message in the classifieds section read, "Oops" about leaving them out and blamed it on faulty glue. Since I was among the most reliable writers – I never missed a deadline – whoever was editor, kept space for my column.

As my column gained in popularity, the scope of my coverage increased. I began writing restaurant reviews. As a "celebrity" in the community, I was asked to emcee small events and fundraisers. I found that I had a natural ability in front of a crowd. I'd always been quick with a wisecrack or pun and got laughs when hosting events. I have always been punctual and reliable, two rare traits in the kind of folks who host bar events. I was a queen who would show up on time and be sober! That added to my appeal with event organizers and requests for appearances increased.

Since my social life was now centered around the gay community, I moved from Chicago's primarily residential northwest side to New Town. This is where most of Chicago's gay community lived. New Town is now known as Lakeview or Boy's Town.

After child support, my net income was $150 a week. That didn't leave much for rent and according to the divorce settlement, I couldn't live with another man. So, I had to settle for an apartment at Dakin and Fremont, a dangerous area at the time. My $175 a month apartment was huge and sunny. It was also cockroach-infested, the windows leaked when it rained, was prone to break-ins, and I chased hookers out of the vestibule all the time. I lasted three months before I moved out and slept on my grandmother's sofa.

I eventually offered my grandmother a deal. If she gave me what she had saved for my inheritance, I would use it as a down payment on an apartment building. We could live in our own apartments, and she wouldn't have to pay rent, only utilities, and I'd be nearby to take her shopping and run errands. My share of the inheritance wasn't enough, so my parents went in with us and we bought a three-flat on Southport near Belmont.

My grandmother lived in the first floor two-bedroom apartment. I lived in the one-bedroom garret, and we rented out a three-bedroom unit on the second floor, which paid the entire mortgage. That area is now a hip, trendy place to live. However, back in the late 1970s it was poor working-class white folks and old people, but it was close to public transportation and the gay neighborhood.

I began volunteering at Gay Horizons, a gay social services agency, answering the crisis hot-line and running "coming out" workshops. During that time, I made several friends, mostly other volunteers. Four of us became close friends. I was in my late 20s, the other volunteers in their late teens or early 20s.

Socially, they were more experienced than I was. I am still friends with Kelvin Harris and Paul Escriva, two of our group from that time. Our friend, Ben Baily, passed away from complications of diabetes and obesity. I joke that we were the original *Sex in the City* girls – I was Carrie!

Ben had a small, cluttered basement apartment. Paul lived in a tiny, but immaculate, studio. Kelvin had a great apartment, but in a horrific neighborhood, where he was burglarized continuously. Kelvin came to stay on the sofa-bed in my living room while he looked for a new space to live. My wife couldn't object because Adam was staying at my grandmother's apartment on the weekends. Kelvin and I got along so well that that "temporary" arrangement lasted for years.

The others had been out since their teens or college years. I had missed that, but now I experienced the adolescence and hedonistic ways most people go through during college and soon after. However, my feelings of inadequacy about my looks and weight – I had a 30" waist which I stuffed into 29" Jordache Jeans! – kept me from being as sexually free as my contemporaries. We'd go out every weekend hitting the clubs. Chicago was different from many other cities in that its nightclubs, at least the gay ones I went to, didn't charge a cover, or only a minor one. I allowed myself $3 to spend for the evening. Not only did it permit me to go out when I had little discretionary income, I usually didn't drink enough to get drunk.

The exception to that was Tuesday nights at Broadway Limited. It was a buck to get in, but after that all drinks were a quarter, so my three dollars went a long way. I went in to work hungover many a Wednesday! Broadway Limited was on the second floor above a collection of storefronts. You entered a narrow stairway between two passenger train cars, converted into the dining room of a restaurant. That set of stairs took you up to a casual lounge area and beyond that was a large dance floor and bar. There was another set of stairs that served as the exit, but the place was a firetrap. Luckily there never was a fire, but Ben, Paul, and Kelvin needed to get me a little tipsy before we even got there. I have always had an unreasonable fear of getting caught in a fire. No childhood trauma to cause that, but there it was and remains still.

I continued mailing in my "Gay Gourmet" column and had little interaction with the people in the office. By then, my ex-wife had remarried, and she and her husband lived on the far northwest side, about an hour's bus ride from my apartment on Southport. My full-time job as a Child-Life Therapist – now at Rush Hospital instead of the University of Chicago – meant that I primarily worked with terminally and chronically ill children. I was exhausted by the end of my workday and eventually, when the job proved too draining, I quit and applied for unemployment.

I was always open about being gay with Adam, as much as he could understand for his age. He met my friends and I took him to events in the community, especially the gatherings the gay parents' group hosted. He grew up having friends with gay parents and it never seemed odd to him. He knew some people didn't understand or accept me, and he quickly learned with whom he could share that part of his life. He also realized I hadn't come out to my grandmother and he kept that from her.

Another fact he kept from me is that his stepfather beat him with a belt. Adam didn't reveal this to me at the time – he told me nearly 40 years later. When his mother remarried, she and her husband put Adam in a Catholic school. He had a hard time fitting in. The majority of the kids were blond and Polish, and a little dark-skinned brown-haired kid was just prime for teasing. He got into a lot of fights.

One day my ex-wife called and asked me to talk to Adam – the kids were teasing him about his gay father, and he was getting into fights. I picked up Adam from school, and on the bus ride home we had a long talk. I asked him what was going on. That's when Adam told me the kids weren't teasing him about me, but about his stepfather. They thought his stepfather was gay. It was all I could do not to laugh out loud.

That story became one I told at parties, and it always got a big laugh. Especially since my ex-wife's husband was a big burly guy, not the stereotypical idea of a gay man. When Adam told me about his stepfather beating him with a belt, I was shocked and angry. I thought this man had been a loving parent to my child. How could I have been so blind? Adam explained that it only happened once, and he told his grandmother – my ex-wife's mother – and she intervened. According to Adam, the police were called, and his stepfather never touched him again. Adam also told me he was teased at school because of me. But that he didn't want to hurt my feelings by telling me. Forty years later, we were able to talk it out, but I still have heartache that my little boy felt he had to protect me that way. I wish I had known.

# PAPER CUTS

Soon after that incident, Adam came to stay with me for more extended periods. Every week I picked him up after school on Friday and dropped him off Monday morning. I was so happy to have the extra time with him that I didn't question why even though I should have been suspicious. I had a one-bedroom apartment but my grandmother's apartment downstairs had two bedrooms, so that's where Adam slept. On the weekends, in the evening, I took him downstairs to spend time with my grandmother before I put him to bed. I was then free to go out and socialize with the friends I'd made at Gay Horizons. In the morning, my grandmother made breakfast for Adam before he came back upstairs to my place.

# CHAPTER 4

When out in the community, people often told me about recipes they'd tried and suggested I feature them in the column. It amazed me how important it was for people to see their names published in the paper. I decided to host a cook-off as a way to share their recipes. The cook-off was held at a bar called Norma's, on N. Halsted St. Although we only had a few entries, the people attending had a great time. The event was a big success and became an annual event that ran for about five years. Joining me as a judge was a new friend of mine, Marty Gigele, owner of Zazoo's, a gay restaurant in Andersonville. The other judges were Norma, who owned the bar bearing her name, and Ron Helizon, also known as the Polish Princess. Ron wrote the bar news and gossip column for *GayLife*.

I don't know how Ron Helizon became affiliated with *GayLife*, but he did have the gift of gab and could get anyone to talk to him. Somehow, he always knew what was going on before anyone else. A great talent to have if you're writing a gossip column. He was a sweet and charming man but struggled to arrange words into a readable sentence. He also battled alcoholism his whole life.

# Ron Helizon

Ron Helizon, 65, passed away due to complications of a stroke on March 6, 2011. He was the beloved partner of Gordon Burrows.

Known as "The Polish Princess," Helizon was a popular bar owner and community activist for several decades. He was especially vocal in Catholic gay outreach as a member of the Archdiocese Gay and Lesbian Outreach (AGLO).

Helizon owned the gay bar Company from 1983-1994, on Halsted just south of Diversey. It was a bar that welcomed LGBTs of all backgrounds and held many benefits for gay and AIDS groups.

Helizon was born in Chicago on October 25, 1945. He attended Holy Innocents grammar school and remembered being taunted for being effeminate. After experiencing harassment for being gay, he was kicked out of Cathedral High School and finished his education at Wells High School.

"When I got asked to leave high school, it took me a while before I could go back to mass," Helizon said in an interview. "Because I love mass, I love my faith, I love praying. I just do. I finally went back, and I reconciled. I realized that it wasn't the being, it was the people." He was told about a welcoming Catholic group, Dignity/Chicago which met at the old St. Sebastian's, at Halsted and Wellington. "I walked in there, and when I walked in, I thought I had met Jesus Christ personally."

Helizon was committed from that point to changing the church from within. He joined Dignity's board and years later when Dignity was forced to split by the Catholic Church, when AGLO was formed, Helizon joined the new Catholic Church-sanctioned AGLO. He was involved with them for two decades in numerous roles.

Helizon participated in pride parades and protests, including the 1970s protest against Anita Bryant at Medinah Temple, where he said he proudly carried the Dignity banner.

*GayLife* newspaper also ran a gossip column by Ron Helizon during the 1970s, when the paper was owned by Grant Ford.

Source: Windy City Times, March 6, 2011

Every Monday he dropped off a pile of cocktail napkins with notes scribbled onto them. Sarah, Steve and whoever else was in the office, deciphered the scribblings, trying to make sense of them for his column. Since there wasn't much to go on, it consisted of short sentences, like, "Chuck Renslow is thinking of opening a new bar," or "Michael Shimandle is now working at Buddies." I occasionally helped compile the column and adopted a breezy style of short statements. A style similar to Walter Winchell's society column, not that I had ever read them. My entire knowledge of his columns came from seeing him portrayed in old movies and TV shows.

I liked the column so much that I started writing my own version called "Gays of Our Lives," which I submitted in small paragraphs for *GayLife*'s free classifieds. It mostly featured the friends I made at Horizons. I would make up the most outlandish things about them; if one went out and bought a new pair of jeans, I described it as "whirlwind shopping spree." Since having their names appear in a gay publication could mean them losing their jobs, I assigned everybody society-column style names. My friend Paul Escriva became Lady Caroline Worthington III, Ben Bailey became Charlotte Webb, and my roommate Kelvin Harris was Miss Peaches. We had great fun with it. What I didn't realize was that "Gays of Our Lives" was gaining a following – readers thought the characters were real people.

The classifieds in *GayLife* had another significant impact on my life. The script that I wrote based on my friends' songs continued to develop in the back of my mind. Even though they moved away, and we drifted apart, I still thought it was a good concept for a musical. I placed a classified ad seeking a songwriter. I spoke to a few people. One man and I hit it off immediately. We met, he loved the script and within a few weeks we were collaborating. His name was Frank DePaul. I began revising my initial script; he wrote new songs and we co-wrote the lyrics. In Frank, I found a soul mate. It was never romantic, more fraternal – or what I imagined camaraderie with brothers would be like, as I never got along with either of mine. In my grandiose dreams, I imagined we could become the next Rodgers and Hart or Kander and Ebb. We met several times a week to work on our play, now called *Spin Cycle*.

Since I wasn't in the *GayLife* office daily, I was unaware of the machinations and office politics taking place, nor was I aware of the financial struggles. Grant Ford was a wonderful man, but at that time, as now, running a gay publication was a struggle. He founded *GayLife* on a shoestring and that string was becoming frayed. Some weeks, the only reason the paper hit the streets was sheer determination and the goodwill of Fred Eychaner who owned the printing press. Grant, who had turned over leadership of the paper to others when he ran for alderman, began to find his interest in running the paper dwindling. During one of the many financial crises, he accepted a loan from Chuck Renslow, who owned a leather bar and bathhouse among other businesses.

It's no exaggeration to say that few people have had as much influence over Chicago's LGBTQ community as Fred Eychaner and Chuck Renslow. Both were recognized for their contributions with inductions into Chicago Gay & Lesbian Hall of Fame; Renslow in 1991 and the more low-key Eychaner in 2015.

## Fred Eychaner

Fred Eychaner, 70, chairman of Newsweb Corporation, President of Alphawood Foundation, for his philanthropy, his public service, and his support of Chicago's LGBT communities.

Fred Eychaner is chairman of Newsweb Corporation and President of Alphawood Foundation. In 2014, he was included in *Chicago* magazine's list of the 100 most influential Chicagoans. He is known for his philanthropy in the city, especially his support of LGBT organizations, HIV support organizations, arts institutions, public spaces, and historic preservation.

Eychaner was born in DeKalb, Illinois, in 1944. He attended the Medill School of Journalism and founded Newsweb Corporation, which prints a variety of newspapers, in 1971. A series of negotiations subsequently led to his acquisition of WPWR–Channel 50, which he sold in 2002. In 2005, he launched WCPT-AM, Chicago's progressive talk radio station.

Throughout several political cycles, Eychaner has been a top Democratic donor; in the 2012 election cycle he was the top contributor to Democratic Super PACs. Many of his political donations have been made in support of LGBT rights, in particular the drive for marriage equality in Illinois. A great deal of the LGBT infrastructure in Chicago bears his stamp. He is the largest donor to the AIDS Foundation of Chicago and has been instrumental in the creation and ongoing viability of a number of the most influential LGBT rights organizations in the state.

In 2014, Eychaner received the Lambda Legal National Liberty Award, which represented the first time that this prestigious honor has recognized an individual outside of New York or Los Angeles. In his acceptance speech, he looked back on more than forty years of LGBT progress, from those who resisted the police at Stonewall, to members of ACT UP fighting for their lives against HIV and AIDS, to the lesbians who gave blood when gay men could not, to the hatred spawned by Reagan-era Republicans, to Irwin Keller and Jonathan Katz of Gay and Lesbian Town Meeting fighting for rights in Chicago in the 1980s, up to the recent struggle to win marriage equality.

"Always remember, never forget," he chanted at several points. For Eychaner, the evening offered a chance not only to celebrate successes but also reflect on the many gains have been won in a spirit of unity and togetherness. "The grassroots process," he recalled. "Fighting in the trenches, one phone call at a time. There was a time when most Americans did not know that they knew an LGBT person. The process of coming out; coming out to friends, our family, our coworkers has led us to where we are today."

In September 2010, President Barack Obama appointed Eychaner a General Trustee to the Board of Trustees of the John F. Kennedy Center for the Performing Arts. He also serves on the boards of the Joffrey Ballet and of the Art Institute of Chicago and as a trustee of the Asian Art Museum in San Francisco, California.

Source: The Chicago LGBT Hall of Fame website at
glhalloffame.org
Eychaner was inducted in 2015

# CHAPTER 5

As the 1970s turned into the 1980s, I became more involved in volunteering, helping the Gay Parents' Rap Group become an official program of Horizons Community Services. I moved beyond staffing the phones on the crisis line to running Horizons East, a weekly drop-in center and coffee house at the Hull House Center on Broadway and Belmont. During the rest of the week, Hull House served as a community center, running after-school programs for children in the neighborhood. On Friday nights, Horizons took over an upper floor, while the soon to be famous Steppenwolf Theater occupied the building's ground-floor theater. As part of the evening's activities, I arranged at least one workshop or rap session and booked a performer, usually a folk singer. There were also a large number of people who came just to hang out and socialize in a non-bar environment. Many under-age gay kids attended as well. It was one of the few community events not in a bar, and as such, was a place they could meet other gay people. Horizons East lasted a little over a year and never made any money. We were lucky if we broke even, but that wasn't the point anyway. Initiating and running such a successful program, combined with the recognition I was getting for writing the Gay Gourmet column continued to boost my self-confidence. I finally found things I was good at; writing, organizing and running events and programs.

The play Frank DePaul and I wrote, *Spin Cycle*, was produced at the Theater Building on Belmont, just blocks from my apartment. The producer was a woman whom Frank met while directing a play in the suburbs. Unfortunately, it was many years ago, and I can no longer recall her name.

Anyway, she and another person from that group formed Slightly Off-Broadway Productions. It was a small company on a tight budget, one step removed from Mickey and Judy putting on a show in a barn. Still, they managed to get rehearsal space for us, print scripts, pay actors, and hire a photographer to take publicity photos. It felt like legitimate show business to me. I was still collecting unemployment and also worked at my friend Marty Gigele's restaurant, being paid "under the table." So, I was able to devote a great deal of time to the play.

A week after *Spin Cycle* opened, my high school graduating class held its ten-year reunion. I had gotten in touch with a few other people from my class who I'd heard were gay. We asked if we could be seated together. Somehow it got around that we were making a big deal about having a "gay table" and wanted to make a speech at the reunion. That was never our intention; we just wanted to have supportive friends nearby. I did come out in the bio I wrote for the reunion program, so that may have sparked the fear. Oddly enough, years later, I discovered that the woman who made up the story about us making demands was, in fact, a closeted lesbian. Maybe she was worried that we'd force her to sit at our table.

On the day of the reunion, the *Chicago Tribune* ran a review of *Spin Cycle*. It was mostly positive. It was the first time a local gay-themed musical was reviewed by the mainstream press in Chicago. The gay papers made a big deal out of the fact that a "gay" musical was getting a professional production. As I pulled up at my high school reunion in a sports car I borrowed from my mother, I felt like a million bucks. Thank goodness the reunion hadn't been held one day later when the *Chicago Sun-Times* review appeared and completely trashed the show. The reviews for the show were mixed – looking back at the production, rightfully so – but the *Sun-Times* reviewer seemed to have an ax to grind. He was particularly scathing but raved about our leading lady (whom he hit on in an interview he requested). He referred to the plot as "trite." Trite? Just how many musicals had there been about a woman who falls in love with a man who she discovers is gay? Who then becomes her best friend and cabaret partner? While addressing the issues of homelessness and mental health? Keep in mind that this was 20 years before *Will and Grace.*

I had a hit show – *Spin Cycle* was extended five times! My column in *GayLife* was popular, at least the readers' comments made me think so, so I should have been on top of the world. But I was getting uneasy with the paper's new management. Chuck Renslow, who took over control of *GayLife,* had a circle of people around him who referred to themselves as the Renslow Family. It consisted of friends who worked for him in his various businesses, and he began to hire them at *GayLife.* Many of his "family" lived in Renslow's mansion in Lakeview. There were rumors in the community that the family members were Satan worshipers and held S&M orgies. Frankly, they scared me, and I felt wary of working with them. I viewed it as a cult of sorts. Of course, I really didn't know anything about the "family," nor was I friends with anybody involved. I think that, at that time, I was reacting to my own upbringing with a physically and emotionally abusive father, rather than to what was true. I later learned that Chuck was a kind and caring man, devoted to the gay community and his friends.

## Charles "Chuck" Renslow

In the early 1960s he opened the Gold Coast, one of the first openly gay businesses in Chicago and one of the first leather bars in the world. He also published *GayLife,* financially aided many gay rights efforts of the 1960s, 1970s, and 1980s, and has been active in city, state, and national Democratic Party politics. He co-founded the International Mr. Leather contest and set up the Leather Museum and Archives.

A true pioneer in Chicago's gay and lesbian community, Chuck Renslow opened Kris Studio in 1954 and began publishing a variety of male physique magazines. He is considered one of the "old masters" of gay male photography in the United States.

In the early 1960s, Renslow opened the Gold Coast leather bar, one of the first openly gay establishments in Chicago and the nation. By the time it closed in 1987, the Gold Coast was internationally known as the oldest leather establishment in the world. Indeed, its international reputation prompted Renslow to establish another business enterprise.

International Mr. Leather, Inc.™ is an annual celebration. It is recognized as the premier gathering of leather people in the world; it has been estimated to now have a $10 million impact on Chicago tourism.

Renslow's activism and commitment have not been limited to leather. From the early days of his visible presence as a gay businessman, he understood his responsibilities to the larger gay and lesbian population. Renslow has been at the forefront of the political movement toward equal treatment and equal rights. In addition to actively organizing many of Chicago's most recognizable gay and lesbian institutions, he has served as a board member of numerous organizations on the local, national, and international levels. Renslow's involvement has helped to spotlight Chicago and to dispel the myth that all gay life takes place on either the East or West Coast.

As the publisher of *GayLife*, Renslow established a credible voice for Chicago's gay and lesbian community. Combining years of involvement in city and state politics with the then emerging gay and lesbian political presence, he laid much of the groundwork for the community's later achievements in civil rights and equal treatment. Renslow was instrumental in the attainment of numerous milestones. Including the initial introduction of a Chicago gay and lesbian civil rights ordinance and the initial executive order banning discrimination in Chicago city government, as issued by Mayor Jane Byrne.

A man of spirituality and belief, he quietly supports the gay and lesbian community and other communities with financial assistance. He is often listed in various program books as Sponsor, Patron, Contributor, or Friend, and his financial and service commitments include most civil rights, environmental and health-related causes in the United States, stretching far beyond the confines of the gay and lesbian community.

Renslow is the chief executive officer of Renslow Family Enterprises. He is a member of the Strike Against AIDS, Human Rights Campaign Fund, Metropolitan Business Association, Illinois Gay and Lesbian Task Force, National Gay and Lesbian Task Force, National Organization for Women, American Civil Liberties Union, NAACP, Chicago Association of Commerce and Industry, Uptown Chamber of Commerce, 46th Ward Advisory Council, and the 48th Ward Democratic Party Advisory Board.

He has long been active in Chicago's Democratic Party, serving as a precinct captain for eight years in the 43rd Ward, as a candidate for delegate to the 1980 Democratic National Convention, and within the 46th and 48th Ward Democratic Organizations.

Source: The Chicago LGBT Hall of Fame website at
glhalloffame.org
Renslow was inducted in 1991, deceased 2017

The few times I was in the *GayLife* office, it was apparent that Sarah and Steve were no longer in charge. Eventually, Sarah left to found her own typesetting company. Steve still worked for the paper, he had a position at city hall's news desk and was seldom around the office. As part of the change-over, Renslow hired a new editor, Albert "Bill" Williams. Where Sarah and Steve had been friendly and welcoming, Bill was pompous and officious. When I dropped off my column, his gruff manner made me feel as if I were bothering him and that my contributions weren't valued. In the past, I would have just accepted it, but with my new-found self-confidence, it began to irritate me.

## Albert N. Williams

Since 1970, as journalist, theater artist, teacher, and activist, he has made important contributions to Chicago cultural life. His *Chicago Reader* theater reviews won a George Jean Nathan Award, and in the 1980s he was an award-winning editor of *GayLife* and *Windy City Times* newspapers. He has performed and written for musical theater and participated in activist groups. He also teaches at Columbia College.

As journalist, theater artist, teacher, and activist, Albert Williams has made important contributions to the cultural life of Chicago.

Prominent as an openly gay writer in the gay, lesbian, bisexual and transgender (GLBT) press as well as the non-GLBT press for more than 30 years, he has been chief theater critic of the *Chicago Reader* weekly newspaper since 1991.

His *Reader* reviews earned him the prestigious 1999-2000 George Jean Nathan Award for Dramatic Criticism from the heads of the English departments of Cornell, Princeton, and Yale universities. As the only Chicago-based critic to have won that national prize, he received letters from Mayor Richard M. Daley and city Cultural Affairs Commissioner Lois Weisberg honoring him as a leading cultural figure in the city. The selection committee wrote: "Albert Williams writes the kind of criticism for which the George Jean Nathan Award was designed – incisive, thorough, confident in the intelligence of its readers, and convinced that theatre makes a difference to the city in which it occurs. ... This is generous and fair-minded reviewing, achieving a consistently high quality."

Williams has also written for the *New York Times Book Review*, the *Advocate*, *Entertainment Weekly*, *American Theatre*, the *Boston Herald*, the *New Art Examiner*, *Stagebill*, the *Chicago Sun-Times*, the *Chicago*

*Tribune*, *GayLife*, *Windy City Times*, the *Chicago Free Press*, and the *Chicago Seed*. He was managing editor of *GayLife* from 1981 to 1985 and represented the Chicago weekly paper at the 1982 Washington, D.C. conference of activists and health professionals at which the name Acquired Immune Deficiency Syndrome (AIDS) was designated for what was then called GRID (Gay-Related Immune Deficiency). He was the only member of Chicago's GLBT press to cover that landmark event in person. Williams also served as managing editor of *Windy City Times* in 1987. He has received two Peter Lisagor Awards from the Chicago Headline Club (local chapter of the Society of Professional Journalists) for arts criticism and reporting in *Windy City Times* (1991) and the *Reader* (2000). His simultaneous involvement in both the GLBT and general-interest press has helped to pave the way for openly gay and lesbian writers in Chicago's mainstream media.

From 1970 to 1974, Williams was a performer and writer with the Free Theater, one of the seminal ensembles in Chicago's off-Loop theater movement. Besides performing, he co-wrote several musical theater works, including the libretto for a children's opera, William Russo's *The Golden Bird*, which premiered in 1984 at Orchestra Hall under auspices of the Chicago Symphony Orchestra. In 1985, he co-produced *Arts Against AIDS*, a benefit show at Second City that launched what would become the AIDS support agency Season of Concern. Williams has also held leadership positions with the Chicago Lesbian and Gay International Film Festival, the Gay and Lesbian Town Meeting, the Coalition Against Media/Marketing Prejudice, and other cultural and political groups. A 1973 graduate of Chicago's Columbia College, Williams has served on the Columbia faculty since 1985, teaching theater and music and advising on GLBT issues.

Source: The Chicago LGBT Hall of Fame website at
glhalloffame.org
Williams was inducted in 2004

One day, soon after *Spin Cycle* opened, I dropped off my column at the *GayLife* offices, where Bill Williams was as brusque as usual. He may have been overwhelmed with work, but I took it personally. On the way to the bus, I picked up a new publication, *Gay Chicago*. It was primarily a bar guide, listing drink specials, parties at the bars and things like that. I read it as I rode the #22 Clark St. bus to my apartment in Lakeview. I happened to look at the masthead address, just as we were approaching the stop closest to its office. I got off the bus and walked two blocks over to the magazine's office on Wells Street. The address was for a storefront with apartments above. I double-checked the address, thinking I made a mistake, but it was correct. Then I discovered a side door and a bell listing Gernhardt Publications. I rang it, and when the buzzer sounded, I opened the door and walked up a steep flight of stairs.

I opened the door and saw the spaces intended to serve as the living and dining rooms of the apartment filled with desks, all shrouded under a cloud of cigarette smoke. A drag queen wearing a lot of make-up asked me if she could help me. I soon realized that she was a real woman, just heavily made up. I explained that I wanted to speak to the publisher. When Dan Di Leo came over, I introduced myself. To my surprise, he knew who I was. I hesitantly asked if he would be interested in running my column in *Gay Chicago*.

He answered, "Yes!" with such enthusiasm that I was taken aback. He went into an adjacent room and brought out Ralph Paul Gernhardt, his co-publisher, who seemed equally eager to have me write for their magazine. Dan then asked me how much I charged. Since I had never been paid, I didn't have any idea what to ask, so I asked them to make me an offer.

"How's $25 a column?" Dan asked, somewhat apologetically.

I was blown away. At that time I was making about $200 from unemployment, with $50 of that going to pay child support. Money was so tight, that I ate stir-fried cabbage and ramen noodles five or six nights a week. I only allowed myself one wine spritzer when I went out clubbing. After one drink, I'd pick up an empty beer bottle and hold it all night. That amount of money coming in every week would be a big help financially. Of course, I agreed.

"Hopefully, we'll be able to increase that soon," said Ralph as he introduced me to the staff of the magazine. It was a very different atmosphere from the offices at *GayLife*. Most everybody worked in one big room, whereas *GayLife*'s space was a maze of individual offices. It turned out that the woman who had greeted me was the publication's typesetter, Karen Ross-Triner. Karen, while identifying as straight, had many friends in the gay community. She'd bartended at a couple of gay bars, and her husband had worked as a DJ at one of them. I also met Michael Williams, who was Ralph's lover and worked doing the production of the magazine.

At that time, production consisted of actually pasting copy, pictures, and ads onto boards, called flats, which were then sent to the printer. I had done that kind of work on my high school yearbook and during college at a couple of part-time gigs at local printers and for *Time* magazine. The staff was on deadline, and I didn't have to pick up my son until the next day, so I offered to help. I immediately felt as if I belonged to what seemed like one big happy family. As it turned out, the staff *was* a big happy, if sometimes dysfunctional, family. It's ironic that because of my fears and prejudices, I was worried about being swept up in the Renslow Family. Yet, I joined Ralph, later nicknaming him, Big Daddy. Ralph and his group were just as tight-knit as Renslow's.

Dan Di Leo, who had been a reporter in Milwaukee, had to leave that city after being caught having sex with an underage youth. He arrived in Chicago, met Gernhardt and joined the staff as co-publisher in 1977, bringing to the paper his expertise in reporting. Di Leo was responsible for the editorial content of *Gay Chicago*, as well as the publication's business matters.

Following Di Leo's death, Gernhardt hired Jerry Williams as business manager and eventual co-publisher. Williams left the magazine under a cloud of suspicion after rumored financial irregularities. Although Gernhardt hired Stacy Bridges as an ad salesman and eventual co-publisher, *Gay Chicago* never regained financial stability. Although the publication experienced tough times, Gernhardt continued to publish until his death at 72 in 2006.

After Gernhardt's death, his son Craig took over. *Chicago Reader*'s Michael Miner, in an article titled "The final days of *Gay Chicago*" wrote that the magazine had run up a massive debt with its printer, Newsweb. And, that they were coming after Gernhardt Publications in court. "A default judgment of more than $95,000 loomed." Gernhardt tried several schemes and last-ditch attempts to save the magazine, but it ceased publication in September of 2011.

## Dan Di Leo

Dan Di Leo (1938-1989), a U.S. Army veteran and co-founder of *Gay Chicago*. His experience and knowledge as a journalist and businessman were largely responsible for the early growth of the magazine, which is a cornerstone of Chicago's LGBT community. He died of complications from AIDS.

*Gay Chicago* co-founder Dan Di Leo moved to Chicago in 1977 and shortly afterward began working as a typesetter and editor for Ralph Paul Gernhardt's *Gay Chicago News*, the first weekly publication serving what was then "Chicago's lesbigay community." When, a few months later, that struggling newspaper ran into financial difficulties, Di Leo – who was a military veteran and an experienced journalist – became, with Gernhardt, a partner and co-publisher of *Gay Chicago*.

Di Leo was a fighter throughout his life. Born at Cook County Hospital in 1938, at the age of 6 he was placed in foster care and lived with more than a dozen families in northern Illinois and southeastern Wisconsin. He attended Marquette University in Milwaukee and, while still a student, began his newspaper career at the *Milwaukee Sentinel*. After being drafted into the military in 1961, he served two years at Fort Carson, Colorado, before re-enlisting and taking an assignment as an interpreter and intelligence agent in West Berlin, where he also worked for *The Berlin Observer*, an English-language newspaper. After leaving military service in 1967, Di Leo held a variety of editorial positions at the *Decatur Herald* and *Rockford Morning Star*. Upon moving to Chicago, he became a copy editor at the *Chicago Sun-Times*.

Di Leo's experience, knowledge as a journalist, and experience as a businessman were largely responsible for the early growth of *Gay Chicago*, which remains strong to the present day. In the years when Di Leo and Gernhardt published the magazine (along with *Gay Detroit*, *Gay Ohio*, *Midwest Times*, and *Gay Milwaukee*, none of which lasted very long), they worked to build *Gay Chicago* and increase the staff of journalists to meet the demands of changing times. The two men learned from each other and taught their staff lasting lessons in editorial and business honesty, integrity, and ethics.

Di Leo was one of the founders of Strike Against AIDS and the Mr. Windy City contest. He was also one of the original contributors to Howard Brown Memorial Clinic, now the Howard Brown Health Center.

For the last years of his life, Dan Di Leo lived with AIDS, fighting opportunistic illnesses one by one and succeeding beyond the expectations of medical authorities. He succumbed to his illness in 1989, but his memory lives on, both in the Chicago community and in the enduring strength of *Gay Chicago*.

Source: The Chicago LGBT Hall of Fame website at
glhalloffame.org
Di Leo was inducted in 2004, deceased 1989

# Ralph Paul Gernhardt

Ralph Paul Gernhardt has fostered the development and cohesion of Chicago's sexual-minority communities by helping to provide them for nearly three decades with the news and information vital to any community's growth.

In 1975, building on his radio broadcasting background, Gernhardt launched a telephone information line that was updated daily. Then, in 1976, he took the next step and started publishing in print. This led to the birth of *Gay Chicago News*, the first weekly publication for lesbian, gay, bisexual, and transgender (LGBT) Chicagoans, for which Gernhardt hired Dan Di Leo, an experienced newspaperman, as writer and editor.

Six months later in 1977, Gernhardt and Di Leo (who died at age 51 in 1989) became business partners and co-publishers of *Gay Chicago*. It is still appearing weekly as Chicago's longest-lived LGBT publication and itself entered the Chicago Gay and Lesbian Hall of Fame in 1989.

Gernhardt was born on Chicago's North Side in 1934. After graduating from high school in Fox Lake, he enlisted in the U.S. Air Force, serving as a special weapons technician and observer in post-war Korea. Finishing his four-year tour of duty in Wyoming, he returned to Chicago and completed training for a radio broadcasting career. His 17-year radio career included work in Michigan, Wyoming, Colorado, Louisiana, Texas, and Tennessee. In 1959 he married Marilyn Ridgedale, and the couple had two children, Craig and Christy. While working in Nashville, Tennessee, Gernhardt gained custody of the children and, in the early 1970s, moved back to Chicago to be near his family. Here, he taught radio broadcasting before starting his LGBT career.

During that career, besides publishing, Gernhardt became an organizer of the Gay Athletic Association, which preceded the current Chicago Metropolitan Sports Association. He and Di Leo also sponsored numerous bowling and softball teams. They were founding members of the Gay and Lesbian Press Association. Using *Gay Chicago* pages, they tirelessly promoted safer-sex practices. They supported anonymous HIV testing programs, and distributed free condoms in addition to publishing a Safe Sex Calendar. With Robert Fagenholz and his son, Fred, of the recently closed Marigold Bowling Arcade, they formed "Strike Against AIDS," a group that contributed tens of thousands of dollars to fight AIDS. Gernhardt's support of AIDS work, athletics, and community events (such as an annual Gay Day at the Great America amusement park) continues today.

Gernhardt's career has also included presenting the "Gay Chicago

Awards" from 1977 to 1992, which honored outstanding achievements by community members in those years. He has aided fundraising efforts for the Center on Halsted activities and continues to be a productive, contributing Chicagoan.

Source: The Chicago LGBT Hall of Fame website at
glhalloffame.org
Gernhardt was inducted in 2004, deceased 2006

# CHAPTER 6

Within the decade since graduating high school, I had gotten married, come out to my wife, gotten separated and divorced from her, changed careers, had a play produced, found my place in the gay community and was in a happy place in my life. Or, I should say, I was often in a happy place. Although I didn't know it at the time, I am bipolar. I'd be happy, amazingly productive, and busy, almost maniacally so. Then in the blink of an eye, I was so depressed that I just wanted to withdraw from everyone.

This had happened to me throughout my life. I'd be fine one minute and fighting back tears the next. Or I'd be in a store and have a disagreement with a salesclerk and feel consumed by intense anger. I'd always been able to control myself but would find myself in the car screaming at the top of my lungs. I was always ashamed of my feelings and tried to keep them suppressed. However, these mood swings were coming more often and becoming more severe.

I was at a record store that offered one-hour free parking. When I left, there was a line of cars waiting to leave the lot. When I finally reached the gate, I handed the attendant my ticket and started to drive away. She insisted I owed money because I was in the lot two minutes over the allotted time. I pointed out that I'd been waiting in line before my time expired, but she was insistent.

I yelled at her, stepped on the gas, and drove through the mechanical arm blocking my way. The entire way home, I was shaking, and certain the police would pull me over. I pulled into my garage, went up to my attic apartment, and told myself I'd been justified in my behavior, that the attendant was being unreasonable.

A few weeks later, I was at home alone, Kelvin was working, and Adam was at his mother's house. I was folding laundry when I felt a wave of sadness engulf me. It was far worse than anything I'd experienced before. At times I would feel melancholy, but this time I was crying; big chest-heaving-tears-rolling-down-my-face sobs. I thought about my recent behavior at the parking lot and was so filled with shame. I walked into the kitchen and took a knife from the drawer. I had the knife at my wrist and was about to slit it when I realized that if I killed myself, Adam would have no one other than my ex-wife in his life.

I put the knife down and called a friend of mine, John Rouse, who was a psychotherapist. John kept me talking for 20 minutes before putting his lover Kevin on the phone to talk to me until he could get to my house. When John arrived, we talked for more than an hour. I told him everything; all the shame and the anger at my father for mistreating me so badly, and at my mother for allowing him to do so. Even though I never hit or belittled Adam, I told John about my fears of doing so. At the end of that hour, after he talked me off the metaphorical ledge, John told me to come see him for a session the next day. He also sent me to my medical doctor for blood tests. I ended up on medication to help control my bipolar disorder. After a couple years of therapy, I was doing much better. It was good that I started seeing John because I was about to enter a very stressful time in my life.

# CHAPTER 7

In the April 22, 1982 edition of *Gay Chicago*, the same issue in which Ralph and Dan announced I was joining the staff, there was an article about the opening of the new musical, *Scrapbook*. The second collaboration I had with Frank DePaul. *Scrapbook* was what is now referred to as a "jukebox musical." It was written before I – or most anyone else – had a computer and the script is long lost. I'd love to be able to see it again to see if it holds up. I was very proud of that script. It told the story of five characters who lived through the early '60s and into the '80s. Each of the characters started out as an archetype – cheerleader, jock, stoner, prom queen, church girl. The play opens with each character addressing an imaginary group – the cheerleader her squad, the jock his teammates, etc. Each monologue overlaps the previous one with opening and closing lines that are identical and spoken in unison. During the play we see each character on their journey as they develop into fully realized personas. Each scene concludes with a song from the era. The show got excellent reviews and ran for about two months.

Our producer for *Scrapbook* and *Spin Cycle* decided that the stress of the job was too much for her. She signed over the rights to the company, Slightly Off-Broadway Productions, to Frank and me. We put together a board of directors, including Frank's boyfriend at the time, Scott Mullen. After

*Scrapbook* Frank and I worked on another jukebox show, *Ladies at Large*. It all began when an actress friend complained that she was never cast as an ingénue or leading lady, so she never sang the best songs. Frank and I came up with the idea to write a show in which larger women would sing the songs usually sung by the romantic leading lady. We cast the show first. After working with these women in a series of workshops, we wrote the script based upon their experiences. It wasn't great theater, but it was fun. The show had a respectable run and even made a profit for our company. We had nearly $2,000 in the company account, which felt like a fortune at the time.

While that show was running, Frank and I worked on an idea that came to me in a grocery store. At that time, grocery stores were introducing generics. Canned vegetables, pasta, and other products sold in plain packages, usually with black and white printing, a no-frills product cheaper than brand names. It triggered the idea of writing a generic musical, spoofing the tropes of the genre. We began working on *Musical* in 1981.

We finished writing the show, had a couple of staged readings, then I left town for a short break. When I returned, I discovered money missing from the company's bank account. Meanwhile, Frank and Scott found the money to rent a luxurious apartment in Marina Towers, which at the time, was considered a very up-market place to live. I asked Frank and Scott for an explanation – they claimed they were owed money for work they did for the company. I feared the worst. I checked our bank accounts and they had embezzled almost everything. I felt betrayed and angry. I closed down the bank accounts, dissolved the company and had nothing to do with them.

Around that time, my divorce was finalized, and I was forced to come out to my grandmother. I was shocked by her reaction. With a disgusted look on her face, she told me I was sick. It was the first hurtful experience I'd had in coming out. Usually I checked on her every day, but after what she said, I was so angry I didn't check on her for a few days. During that time, she had a stroke. A neighbor found her, and she was rushed into hospital, then to a nursing home. She lost the ability to speak or communicate. I visited her and tried to apologize. All I saw was disappointment behind her clear, blue eyes. I hugged her, but her arms lay limp. I didn't know if she was physically incapable or whether she couldn't stand to be near me. She died soon afterward. I felt responsible. Even though she was in her 80s and nearly 100 pounds overweight,

I thought she'd live forever. For years thereafter, I had nightmares and would wake up in a panic. Several times I actually reached for the phone to call her.

With my grandmother dead, my ex-wife knew that Adam no longer had a bedroom in her apartment. Although supportive when I came out to her, she suddenly didn't want me to see Adam at all. She asked me to sign away my parental rights so her new husband could adopt Adam. I told her that would never happen. She filed motions to keep me from seeing Adam. Each time the court appointed a therapist to evaluate my fitness as a parent, she lost. But that didn't stop her from trying. However, in those unenlightened times, the courts ruled that I could see Adam, but only as long as I lived alone.

I had to ask my roommate and best friend Kelvin to find his own apartment. I felt as if my life was crashing down around me. So much of my social life was tied up with the theater company that when it ended, I felt very alone. The only things that kept me going were the desire to be a part of Adam's life and the new writing gig at *Gay Chicago*.

My first column appeared in the May 6, 1982 edition of *Gay Chicago*. In that same issue was an article about the legendary disco, Eddie Dugan's Bistro, being demolished, a victim of gentrification. That area, renamed River North, is now full of trendy restaurants and loft housing. At the time it was gay bars, warehouses, and light industrial businesses. The closing and subsequent demolition of the Bistro coincided with the end of the disco era and the beginning of gay bars and businesses migrating north to Lakeview, a burgeoning gay residential neighborhood.

Soon after I began writing for *Gay Chicago*, I changed my "day job." After I quit working with hospitalized kids, I collected unemployment for a while and worked at my friend Marty's restaurant, Zazoo's. As my unemployment insurance and my time at Zazoo's came to an end, I received a call from the Chicago Board of Education. I took my board exams after graduation, but at the time there was a surplus of teachers and Chicago wasn't hiring. Not owning a car, the suburban schools weren't an option, so I left my name on the list. Finally, they called and I began a 30-year teaching career, all the while working for Chicago's LGBTQ press.

# CHAPTER 8

$$* * *$$

A lthough I no longer wrote for *GayLife*, I was aware of the changes going on there in 1982. In June, Bill Williams was out as editor, to be replaced by Karlis Streips, an activist and recent college graduate. The offices moved again, this time to a property Renslow owned, which also housed Man's Country, a bathhouse. It was rumored that Renslow quashed AIDS coverage because he feared the impact on his businesses, the Gold Coast leather bar, and Man's Country baths. That wasn't the case.

Some in the community pushed him to sell the paper to avoid accusations of conflict of interest. So Renslow encouraged Streips to increase the paper's coverage of AIDS. *GayLife* ran one of its first articles on the mysterious "gay cancer" in the August 6, 1982 issue, marking the first use of the term AIDS in the paper. A week later, a second article ran.

In that same edition, there was a small article quoting a Washington D.C. publication, *Deep Backgrounder*. According to the *Backgrounder*, there were hearings about congressmen sexually harassing their male pages, young interns working in the Capitol. Among those accused was Larry Craig from Idaho who, decades later, was arrested for propositioning an undercover police officer in an Idaho airport.

# PAPER CUTS

After a few months, Karlis Streips found the responsibility of managing all the news coverage overwhelming. Renslow brought back Bill Williams, with Streips stepping aside to serve as Associate Editor. A December '82 issue mentions the death of a celebrity, disco and Hi-NRG dance music composer and recording artist, Patrick Crowley – he worked with Sylvester and Paul Parker. His death was attributed to AIDS. Although AIDS coverage didn't make the front page until January of the following year, from that point on *GayLife* was always at the forefront of reporting about AIDS.

# CHAPTER 9

## ✳ ✳ ✳

After writing a cooking and food-related column at *Gay Chicago* for six months, I was offered the chance to write a review of a gay-themed play. Since I was no longer involved in theater, nor did I think I would ever be again, I felt there was no conflict of interest, so I accepted the assignment. Response to the review was good, and I continued to review plays in addition to my cooking column. I started writing a serialized story in the magazine's classified personal ads, similar to what I had done at *GayLife*, but with a storyline rather than made up gossip items. Again, it was just something to amuse my friends. When I stopped writing it, people wrote and called the offices asking when the story would appear again.

Through working in newspaper publishing, I discovered the world of gay literature. I was always a voracious reader, and in the late–'70s and '80s, the world of gay book publishing was exploding. Two books I read at that time had an impact on me. The first, *Culture Clash* by Michael Bronski made me aware of the gay subtext in much of popular culture. The second was *Tales of the City* by Armistead Maupin, in which there was no subtext; the gay material was front and center.

Maupin's book was a collection of his serialized stories that appeared in the *San Francisco Chronicle* and was a huge seller, leading to a series of books with the same characters. A local Chicago paper had done something similar, called "Bag Time" but, with Chicago being more provincial, there wasn't anything gay about it. Maupin's book inspired me to write my own version in 1984, set in Chicago, with Chicago-centric characters, many of whom were gay. There's a saying, often attributed to Dorothy Parker that, "Imitation is the laziest form of flattery." I wasn't so much imitating Maupin as writing an homage in his style. I was writing it for my own enjoyment when a friend suggested I show it to Ralph and Dan to see if they were interested in running it in the magazine. Ralph and Dan loved it. I handed them thirty chapters, each of which was about one page long. I continued to write the story, letting it take its own course. When the first issue of *Gay Chicago* with "Tales of the Second City" came out, I was surprised to see they ran four chapters. I assumed it was to give the series a jumpstart and they'd drop back to one or two episodes a week.

The response to the series surprised everyone, including me. It was so popular that Dan and Ralph ran numerous chapters each week, using up the material I'd submitted. From that point on, I was struggling to keep up with deadlines. Eventually, it all became too much, and I just ended it. For months afterwards, people called or wrote asking how the story ended. It never occurred to me to submit the story to a publisher. If I had, who knows? I may have become, to coin a favorite phrase of my mother's, "the poor man's" Armistead Maupin.

Years later Maupin was in town to promote his most recent book in the Tales series. I don't recall how I got in contact with him, but I did and asked him to come to a "Meet the Author" party I wanted to throw. To my surprise, he said yes.

I picked him up at Unabridged Bookstore after his signing and brought my idol to my house. The second-floor apartment happened to be vacant at the time. We used that, as well as my apartment upstairs for the event. Maupin couldn't have been more charming or gracious. I'm certain he'd been feted much more luxuriously and spent time with more famous people. Still, he certainly didn't act like he was disappointed. He sat at a small table, signed books, and chatted with everyone for about two hours.

# CHAPTER 10

AIDS and Ronald Reagan dominated the headlines in the 1980s and Reagan is rightfully blamed for his anti-gay/anti-AIDS policies. He allowed AIDS to develop into an epidemic, killing off hundreds of thousands of gay men, before spreading to other communities. However, the 1980s was also a time when gay publishing was thriving. In part because of Reagan's policies. Not that it was his intention, but Reagan inadvertently contributed to the rise of the gay press.

Hundreds of gay newspapers flourished due to a new revenue source that Reagan's economic policies accidentally created. After breaking the AT&T monopoly in 1982 there was a proliferation of independent phone companies offering a variety of services. One industry arising from the deregulation policies was "phone sex" lines. The fear of AIDs was another factor in the vast growth of phone sex lines. Nobody really knew how AIDS was spread. The term "safe sex" hadn't been coined yet. Many men avoided sexual contact with other men, and "phone sex" provided an outlet for their sexual frustration. How could you catch anything? All you were doing was talking on the phone. For the phone sex companies, there was little overhead. However, to make money they had to get lots of people calling in. Many of them advertised in the gay newspapers, providing an influx of capital unprecedented in the gay publishing world.

Established publications, such as *Gay Chicago*, expanded, and new publications popped up regularly. In the '80s *Gay Chicago* grew from a slender magazine of 30-40 pages to nearly 80 pages. Extra pages of advertising meant additional pages of editorial content were needed.

I write quickly – if not always well – and by 1985, *Gay Chicago* was not only running my cooking column and theater reviews, but I was also contributing movie and book reviews. My years of writing gossip columns in the classifieds prepared me for the real thing, and I added another weekly column; a newsy gossip column, "Potpourri." Much of the content of "Potpourri" was a reiteration of events that the bars were hosting or was garnered from press releases. I, however, made it sound like I was giving people the scoop. Much as I did in those classified columns, I would throw in comments about people well known in Chicago's gay community. I made mundane things, such as someone going on vacation, sound like juicy gossip. "Potpourri" became the most popular segment of the magazine – other than the sex ads in the classifieds.

Eventually people called the office and left real gossip on an answering machine – this was long before e-mail. If it was innocuous, or public knowledge, I repeated it. If it was something where I couldn't – or wouldn't – use the person's name, I attributed it to a character I created called Helen Highwater. It was all in good fun, but sometimes I reported something in error, or someone took something meant as a joke seriously. I angered some folks. There was one reader who sent me sheets torn from the magazine, with typos circled in red and nasty comments on the page. I never paid them much mind, but one day I checked my home answering machine to discover a message from a man ranting about me. I was panicked for a bit, then realized that he didn't know he was leaving a message on my line. Instead of having an unlisted number, I had it listed as Helen Highwater. He was ranting about me to the imaginary character I created.

Ralph and Dan were always supportive of whatever I wanted to add to the magazine's focus. *Gay Chicago* was moving beyond just being a guide to drink specials at the bars. It was becoming a features magazine for Chicago's gay community, reporting on life-style concerns. With the increased income from the phone sex ads, Dan and Ralph upgraded the look of the magazine. In April of 1983, they began printing the magazine with four-color glossy covers. The interior was still newsprint, but the covers certainly gave the magazine a more professional look. Unfortunately, Ralph and Dan mis-calculated their increased costs, and it almost bankrupted them. In the July 28, 1983 issue of *GayLife*, there was an announcement that *Gay Chicago* would cease publication. I knew Ralph and Dan were having financial troubles. I offered to write for free until they were back on their feet – not that the one hundred dollars a week I was earning would make much difference. Within a few days, a local businessman, Frank Kellas, invested in the paper and *Gay Chicago* was back on the street, not even missing an issue. Sensing a need in the community, Ralph and Dan decided to take that opportunity to re-launch the magazine with a new focus and a fresh look. Sports, entertainment, and bar news were now collected under a section titled "Out-Look-Out."

Soon after the magazine's re-organization, I woke up in the middle of the night with an idea for a serialized novel. I sketched an outline and proposed it to Dan and Ralph. It was a murder mystery titled "Death on the Rocks." The story featured characters loosely based on celebrities in Chicago's gay community. It featured locales popular with the gay community – bars, restaurant and the landfill area along the lakefront where gay men liked to sunbathe and preen, known as the Rocks. I'd learned my lesson from the last serialized story I'd written. I had all but the final chapter completed before we ran it in the magazine. I wrote the story so that numerous characters had a motive for committing the murders. My concept was that we'd have a contest, and the readers would write the last chapter – or at least explain their reasoning behind "whodunit." Dan and Ralph loved the story but wanted to make it even more interactive. They had the idea of posting clues in various bars and clubs. The winner would have to incorporate at least three of the posted clues in their final chapter. Other clues could be considered red herrings. They got bar and club owners to come on as sponsors – in exchange for free advertising and having the clues posted in their bar.

The serialized mystery developed quite a strong following. About two dozen people submitted a final chapter for the contest. We held a "reveal" party at one of the bars where we announced the winner. We even recruited actors to play out the final chapter, after which we presented the winner with his prize money, which Ralph brought to the event in a briefcase chained to his wrist.

# CHAPTER 11

In 1984 Chuck Renslow hired Tracy Baim, fresh out of college, as an editorial assistant to help expand the paper's coverage. That same year a young, successful commodities trader, Jeff McCourt, approached *GayLife* editor, Bill Williams, about contributing theater reviews. McCourt had no newspaper experience, but he loved theater and attended many productions. *Gay Chicago*'s expanded coverage of nightlife beyond the bars made it a must-read every week. Williams thought he could expand *GayLife*'s readership by covering theater – he was also a bit of a theater buff – and brought McCourt on as an unpaid freelancer. McCourt started writing theater reviews under the pseudonym, Mimi O'Shea. He was immediately seduced by the thrill of the newspaper business, and he took note of the power the publisher of the city's only gay newspaper wielded.

Renslow appreciated his political clout, but also viewed the publication of *GayLife* as a community service; he never thought it could make money. McCourt thought otherwise. He often said, 'I know Chuck thinks the paper can never make money, but I think he's wrong. This kind of a paper could make money if it was marketed right.'"

# Jeffrey E. McCourt

Jeffrey E. McCourt (1955–2007), founding publisher of *Windy City Times*, award-winning journalist, businessperson, and activist, for helping to win mainstream respect and political victories for Chicago's LGBT communities, including passage of the City's 1988 Human Rights Ordinance.

Publisher, businessperson, theater producer, and activist Jeffrey E. McCourt made significant contributions to Chicago and its LGBT communities during the 1980s and 1990s. As founding publisher of *Windy City Times* newspaper, he helped to build a high-quality independent press. Under his leadership, the paper, which McCourt co-founded in 1985 and ran until 1999, nurtured emerging journalistic talent, winning numerous awards for its news coverage and features.

McCourt's standards raised the bar for LGBT newspaper publishing nationwide and led to national advertising contracts with mainstream corporations. He believed that journalists working for the LGBT press should be paid full-time wages in line with daily newspaper salaries. While maintaining *Windy City Times* as an independent voice, he embraced advocacy journalism and supported activism aimed at winning mainstream respect and political victories for Chicago's LGBT communities. During the 1986-'88 stages of a long campaign to pass a Chicago human rights ordinance that would prohibit sexual-orientation discrimination, the newspaper's offices were known as "Ordinance Central" because of McCourt's generosity in allowing activists to use space and equipment. The paper's editorials galvanized community and political support for the ordinance after initial defeats.

Journalist Albert Williams recalled how, in the wake of the ordinance's earlier failure to pass, McCourt's newspaper called Chicago politicians to account. "We were very influenced by the idea that the community needed to take control of our own issues rather than just depending on our friends," he remembered. "Jeff gave the gay and lesbian community a newspaper that was willing to fight." McCourt also supervised *Windy City Times*' investigative reporting into the City of Chicago's funding for AIDS prevention and treatment. After a reporter on the paper revealed that Chicago ranked near the bottom of the top 10 cities in the United States on HIV/AIDS funding, McCourt worked with 46th Ward Alderman Helen Shiller to craft and push through the City Council an ordinance doubling the city's AIDS budget. He was also instrumental in founding the National Gay Newspaper Guild and worked hard to overcome prejudice against the regional gay press within the marketing industry. Besides journalism, McCourt's major passion was for the theater. Prior to *Windy City Times*, he contributed entertainment coverage to Chicago's *GayLife* newspaper. He co-produced the 1994 local premiere of Tony Kushner's *Angels in America* at the Royal George Theatre. He later served as president of the board of American Blues Theatre (now the American Theater Company), where he co-produced a 1997 revival of Lillian Hellman's *Toys in the Attic*. His philanthropic activities included substantial gifts to Children's Place, a pediatric AIDS treatment center, where he also volunteered.

McCourt was born on December 21, 1955, in Newburgh, New York. Prior to his involvement in the newspaper business, he worked in the financial world as an options trader. He died in Chicago of complications from AIDS on March 26, 2007, having distanced himself from LGBT community involvement after selling *Windy City Times* to Tracy Baim, one of the paper's original co-founders, in 2000. Most of his final years were spent at an extended care facility on Chicago's Near North Side.

Source: The Chicago LGBT Hall of Fame website at
glhalloffame.org
McCourt was inducted in 2007, deceased 2007

There was never any animosity or competition between *Gay Chicago* and *GayLife*. We were an entertainment guide, *GayLife* was a newspaper. We each filled our niche and there was plenty of advertising dollars to go around. Of course, our paths crossed at community events and Jeff McCourt was usually the life of the party. While a pleasant enough person, Tracy Baim and I never became close.

In my gossip column, I good-naturedly ribbed McCourt by making comments about his nom de plume, Mimi O'Shea. He – or rather, Mimi – began writing a gossip column as well, and would do the same to me – or rather, Helen Highwater. Some in the community thought we were bitter enemies, sort of Chicago's answer to Hedda Hopper and Louella Parsons, but in fact we were friendly and cordial, sometimes getting together for drinks. We were casual acquaintances, rarely talking shop, usually discussing theater and gossiping. He was a great drinking companion, until the fourth cocktail. Then the nastiness started to flow. That was when I excused myself. Having to be up to teach in the morning was a great excuse.

After working at *GayLife* for less than a year, McCourt was not only contributing reviews, he was the features editor and also in a relationship with the paper's ad sales director, Bob Bearden. He knew exactly how much money was being brought in by ad sales and felt it could be increased. McCourt approached Renslow about buying *GayLife*. Since he had no newspaper experience, Jeff proposed working for Renslow for a year as a kind of internship, at which point he'd purchase the publication.

It didn't take long for Jeff to realize that the newspaper's name, the main "commodity" he would be buying, had been damaged by the controversy over coverage of AIDS. Its leading writer, Steve Kulieke, had moved on to write for the national magazine, *The Advocate*. The only writers of substance at *GayLife* were George Buse, Chris Heim and Marie Kuda. The sole reason to buy the paper would be to gain access to the ad revenue stream. McCourt already had all of the ad contacts since his lover was the ad sales manager. Instead of buying the magazine, he decided to hijack its only tangible assets by enticing a few key staff members to leave with him. This exodus created quite a ruckus in Chicago's press community, both mainstream and LBGT. The following timeline is pieced together from my memories of the event and press reports at the time.

McCourt and Bob Bearden convinced Tracy Baim, along with *GayLife*'s art director, Drew Banadish, to covertly begin a new publication. During the summer of 1985, they planned the deception, allegedly copying ad sales information and sneaking it out little by little. By Labor Day they were ready. McCourt, Bearden, and Badanish each put up $10,000. They put together the new publication in Jeff and Bob's apartment on Melrose Street, just west of Broadway. The offices were upstairs, and the bulky typesetting equipment of the era was kept in the basement.

At the end of September, the foursome stopped showing up at the *GayLife* offices. Chuck Renslow only realized what was happening just below the deadline for the next issue. *GayLife* managed to put out a four-page issue on September 26. The front page detailed the staff walkout. The center spread was pictures, and there were classifieds on the back page. There were no ads and no masthead.

*Windy City Times* debuted on that same date. The first issue was slight, a mere 28 pages, but it featured a headline worthy of a newspaper of its stature, about the formation of Mayor Washington's Committee on Gay & Lesbian Issues (COGLI). Former *GayLife* columnist Jon-Henri Damski also jumped ship and in his initial column did more than a little ass-kiss for his new boss. Referring to McCourt, Damski, wrote, "His only business is this paper and his sole self-serving interest is to put out the best paper possible."

McCourt's "Letter from the Publisher" exhibited his flair for the dramatic, announcing that *Windy City Times* would be, "... a newspaper broad in scope, exciting in presentation, and, above all, honest in its political and social motives. Our ultimate goal is to expand the gay sensibility in positive, progressive directions."

*GayLife* continued to limp along, bringing in Erin Criss as manager, and Jennifer Kapusak as "guest editor." Renslow brought back Karlis Streips as political editor – he had left to attend grad school. The frontpage banner read, "A Decade of Tradition & Integrity." *GayLife* continued for three months before Renslow announced the paper would be published bi-weekly. Only one issue was published after that. *GayLife*'s last issue hit the streets January 13, 1986, five years after Renslow took it over, and less than a year after he hired McCourt and Baim.

The February 13, 1986 issue of *Gay Chicago* featured the reproductions of the first and last *GayLife* front pages. The caption read, "We've lost a good friend ... " Inside, a full editorial page announced the hiring of former *GayLife* staffers as Gay Chicago's ads salesmen and photographers.

# CHAPTER 12

## ✳ ✳ ✳

For the next year or so, both *Windy City Times* and *Gay Chicago* continued to thrive. *Gay Chicago* consistently ran nearly 100 pages an issue. *Windy City Times*, while not as many pages due to its format, was becoming a powerhouse. Both for the quality of reporting and for the high-level advertisers it attracted. Marshall Field's, at that time one of the prime retailers in the Chicago area, began to advertise. Many people are unaware of the significant effect McCourt had on the gay press. He was the first publisher to go after, and get, mainstream corporate advertisers for a gay publication. Before *Windy City Times* most gay press struggled to get by with small ads purchased by bars, restaurants, clothing stores and other local businesses catering to the gay community. *Windy City Times* was the first to run ads by national and international companies: hotel chains, airlines and department stores. He approached these companies as he would any other business and was the first to promote the gay community as an affluent niche market. *Windy City Times* was one of the first gay papers not to use the word "GAY" or a gay symbol in its title, which no doubt helped market it to mainstream businesses.

In a short time, the paper became so profitable, that the newspaper's offices moved out of Jeff and Bob's apartment into a building owned by the Lakeview Mental Health Center. Jeff's alter-ego Mimi O'Shea proudly announced the move in her "Dirt" column, as did I.

I was beginning to be included in upper echelon events in Chicago's nightlife. When Limelight held the grand opening party for its Chicago location in 1985, I received a PR invite. I took my friend Jim Lovette along with me – one of my favorite people. He was a slight man, feminine with bleached hair. As we exited the cab, dressed in festive attire. I was wearing a gold kimono over parachute pants – it was the '80s, what can I say. He was wearing slim-fitting pants and a gauzy, flowing top. When our cab arrived and we exited, we saw a line of people waiting to be allowed entry to the club.

I assumed having a VIP Press invite, I didn't have to wait in line. Jim and I began climbing the steps. Someone in the crowd yelled, "It's the Eurythmics!" Jim did look a bit like Annie Lennox and with my dyed blond hair and beard, I bore more than a passing resemblance to Dave Stewart, the band's other member. The doorman hustled us into the VIP area. When they realized we weren't the famous duo, we were ushered out of the VIP area – so much for my inclusion in the upper echelon. But at least we were allowed to stay in the club.

# CHAPTER 13

✱ ✱ ✱

I was still active with Chicago's Gay and Lesbian Parents' Group. When the group decided to host the Gay Fathers' Coalition International annual conference, I was asked to chair the committee. I had only been to one conference in New York the year before. I had no idea what an undertaking it would be. We booked a hotel near downtown and set up registration, arranged workshops, and brought in speakers and celebrities. At our urging, the Coalition presented its Image in Media Award to *The Tracy Ullman Show*, which featured an ongoing skit about two gay fathers raising a daughter. Character actor Dan Castelanetta, who played one of the fathers (now best known as the voice of Homer Simpson), was a Chicagoan. He and his wife flew in from Los Angeles to accept the award.

I picked Castelanetta and his wife, Deb LaCosta, up at the airport and brought them to the conference hotel in Chicago's then less than trendy West Loop area. I'm confident they were used to much posher transportation and digs, but they were as gracious as could be. They arrived at the conference's gala dinner, sat at the head table and chatted with everyone who came to speak to them. I've since worked with other celebrities, but never met anyone as down to earth and amenable as the Castelanettas.

At that year's conference, our local chapter was able to push through a motion to change the name of the international organization to Gay and Lesbian Parents, instead of Gay Fathers. The name now reflected the membership of the local chapters. That was one of our chapter's goals when we agreed to host the conference.

I was apprehensive about taking the lead role in something that required me to appear before the mainstream news media. Although I was out to family and friends, and some co-workers, speaking to the press meant the parents of my students would also know I was gay. Fortunately, the Chicago Public Schools and Chicago Teachers' Union recently instituted non-discrimination policies.

As I was planning the conference, my parents, who had controlling interest in the building in which my late grandmother and I had apartments, decided to sell the three-flat. I urged them to hold on to the property as the neighborhood was becoming gentrified. My father wanted a quick buck, and my parents sold the building for $25,000 more than they paid for it less than a decade earlier. If they had waited another year, they would have seen nearly a $100,000 profit. I didn't get a penny from them, but I had saved up enough to buy a small one-bedroom condo in Chicago's Margate Park neighborhood.

Although I kept busy, I was desperately lonely. My ex-wife remarried and, even though she had not succeeded in removing Adam from my life, she forced me back into only seeing him every other weekend and Wednesday nights. Even though I was now, effectively single, I had no love life. It turned out that the level of minor celebrity I'd achieved scared many men off. It did attract a particular type – "star fuckers" – men who thought they could climb the gay social ladder by being seen with me. Since I had no real power, they weren't going to get anywhere because of me, except maybe by-passing lines to get into clubs. They soon lost interest. That was fine with me, I was looking for an LTR, long term relationship, in the classified ad parlance of the day.

Since I could run classified ads of any length for free in *Gay Chicago*, I decided to run a personal ad in the relationship section of the magazine, which in those pre-Internet days served the same function as Match.com, Grindr and Craig's List. I carefully crafted a rather lengthy personal ad that began, "Tired of the bars? Well, I'm not! But I am tired of drunks, one-night stands, and attitude. I'm looking for a man to date, with the idea of building a long-term relationship." I made no mention of my role at the magazine, nor did I list my name. The ad continued for a full paragraph, describing my interests and keeping the physical description to a minimum to avoid those who were only looking for sex. I was honest in my brief description of my looks, "I don't stop traffic, but I don't stop clocks." I then took a chance and listed my phone number, followed by, "Serious calls only."

I got more than 200 phone calls in the week the ad ran. About half of those were crank callers or guys looking for sex. But there were quite a few legitimate calls, many of which responded to my humorous tone. When men called, I chatted with them, and if they seemed interesting, I made an appointment to meet them. Always in public places. I was lonely, not dumb. The first man I went out with was delightful. We had a full-fledged date – a picnic dinner during Chicago's Venetian Night boat parade. He could have been "the one." But, since he was the first date, I was honest and said I had a few more people to meet but would like to see him again. He understood and said to call him in a couple of weeks. I then saw 63 other men.

The dates soon dwindled to meeting for coffee or a drink. There were a lot of duds and plenty of men who described themselves inaccurately. One man used the word "nigger" about a dozen times in the first couple of minutes we spoke. Needless to say, he didn't make the cut. In fact, no one matched the connection I felt with my first date. Two weeks later, I called him. He thanked me but said that he'd met someone, and they were in a relationship! I guess I blew that chance.

What was I to do now? I wasn't about to go back to my days of sexual abandon; the AIDS crisis was at its peak. By the end of the year, *Windy City Times'* obits ran more than two pages. So, I threw myself into writing for the magazine. I wrote articles on decorating, entertaining, fashion, even sports. I took part in many benefits and hosted an event welcoming writer Vito Russo, author of *The Celluloid Closet*, who was in town for the opening night of Chicago's Gay & Lesbian Film Festival. Vito and I had a nice little affair that week, then he returned to California and his life there. We remained friends and I was heartbroken when we lost him to AIDS a few years later.

# CHAPTER 14

S oon after *Windy City Times* started publishing, Bob Bearden grew ill. Jeff McCourt didn't want to face it at first, but it soon became evident to others in the community, that Bob had become infected with HIV. A little more than a year later, Bearden died in McCourt's arms. Jeff cried for hours. Yet he managed to write his lover's obituary. It appeared on the front page of *Windy City Times*. He showed great restraint, citing the basic facts of Bearden's life, ending with, "He was admitted to the hospital January 24, 1987, after suffering a brain seizure. He died peacefully in his sleep at approximately 5:30 a.m. January 29, after failing to respond to treatment." His only personal comment was the closing sentence, "His lover, this writer, was at his side at the time of death."

If McCourt harbored doubts about the clout that *Windy City Times* now had, it disappeared in September of 1986 when the paper scored an exclusive, in-depth interview with Mayor Harold Washington. The newspaper was now a political and social force to be reckoned with. Unfortunately, as the paper and Jeff's power grew, so did his ego. When Bearden died, so did some of Jeff's humanity. Maybe Bob served as a buffer, or helped keep Jeff's ego in check, but Jeff became harder and harder to be around. I began to see a nasty side to him and started avoiding him at social events.

He started stirring up trouble just because he could. Local nightclub performer, Pudgy, got her start in Chicago's gay bars and went on to headline in Las Vegas. She was back in town performing at a new nightclub, Byfield's. Pudgy's husband, Mike Cardella, traveled with her and, in addition to serving as a tour manager of sorts, he "served" as her opening act. He was also a former contestant in the Mr. Windy City contest, a beauty pageant for gay men. The contestants were sponsored by gay bars and businesses. Cardella represented a gay bathhouse as Mr. Man's Country. It was one of those times when, in an attempt to be funny, I stepped over the line. In my review of the show, I mentioned Cardella once frequented gay bathhouses. Pudgy was incensed. I met with her and her husband afterward and apologized for upsetting them. While she wasn't happy with my response, she was ready to let the incident drop. However, when Jeff found out about my meeting with them, he made a big deal about it in Mimi's column. People started calling Pudgy and her husband, and I was threatened with a lawsuit. Thankfully, they didn't sue, preferring to let the incident simmer down on its own. Without a legal battle, Jeff had little to report. But it taught me I had to be more circumspect in my comments, my words could hurt. It also showed me how Jeff had changed.

## Pudgy

Female comedy icon Beverly "Pudgy!" Wines died at her home in Las Vegas of a heart attack on Christmas Day, December 25.

She had been appearing as part of a revue at The Flamingo Hotel and was relaxing following two performances. She had also suffered a previous heart attack several years ago.

Wines grew up on Chicago's West Side and worked from coast to coast as well as headlining in Las Vegas; Atlantic City, N.J.; and Reno, Nev., the *Las Vegas Review-Journal* stated.

When Wines began her career as an entertainer, a career that would eventually evolve into "Pudgy! The Queen of Tease," female comics were quite rare. She was frequently compared to fellow female comedians Phyllis Diller and the late Totie Fields. Diller said, "Pudgy was amazingly funny – an original – the perfect person to carry the torch of female comics into the future. There was no one like her. She never used writers. All her material was her own." Unlike most of her "competitors," Pudgy! made her mark without relying on four-letter words or vulgarity. Also, unlike other funny ladies, Pudgy could and sing. In fact, songs were an integral part of her comedy.

Chicago resident and Pudgy! fan Gary Chichester stated to *Windy City Times* that "Pudgy" has always been a friend of Chicago's gay community. From her start as a waitress at the late-night showbiz hangout Punchinello's on Rush to her performance at the first International Mr. Leather, she was always involved with the community both in Chicago and her new-found home in Las Vegas. She will be greatly missed; she was a one-of-a-kind talent.

Source: Windy City Times January 2, 2008

# CHAPTER 15

## ✳ ✳ ✳

**M**y life was fulfilling. I was teaching with people I liked. I also felt I was truly helping the kids. I taught in Cabrini-Green, then one of the most dangerous housing projects in the city. At *Gay Chicago*, I felt like part of a team. I even had my own condo. I was beginning to see Adam more, as my ex-wife allowed me to have him every weekend. He went to one of the city's magnet schools and rode a school bus. Most days the bus picked him up and dropped him off at his mother's house. On Friday, he'd walk from his school, just two blocks from *Gay Chicago*'s office. There he'd sit in Dan's office and do his homework until I arrived from my school, a mile away. On Monday mornings the bus picked him up at my house. I loved it because I got to spend more time with him. What I didn't know at the time was that his mother was shutting him out of her new family – she and her new husband had had a second baby. Adam never mentioned that. He grew up feeling he had to keep things from both his mother and me. For example, he never mentioned to his mother that to walk from his school to the *Gay Chicago* office, where he met me, he passed a dirty bookstore, an adult theater and a hustler bar. I thought he was oblivious, but as an adult he confessed he knew what those places were all along.

One day, as his mother was dropping him off, she handed me a larger than usual bag of his things. She then got out of the car, opened the trunk and pulled out two more large bags and said, "Adam needs to live with you now. He's not working out with my new family," as if he were just a piece of furniture that no longer fit her decor. "Look at it this way," she said, "Now you won't have to pay child support." She waved goodbye to Adam, got in the car and drove away. She hadn't even told him.

I was overjoyed. I loved having Adam live with me, but his "room" in my 600 square foot condo was a fold-out chair-bed behind an L-shaped bookcase. We went out and bought a dresser for his clothes and made do as best we could. Now the school bus picked him up on the corner every day. It wasn't the best area of the city, but he stood right in front of the neighborhood school which did feel safer. It didn't matter what worked best, I had no other options. I didn't know anyone nearby, and I had to be at work an hour before he had to be at school, which had no early drop-off facility. Adam became a latch-key kid. As someone who grew up with a stay-at-home mom, this killed me. He came back from spending the weekend at his mother's house, sullen and angry.

Now I had no time to feel lonely. When we got home from the *Gay Chicago* offices – by bus, I didn't have a car – I made dinner and checked Adam's homework while he was at the neighborhood boy's club. He'd come home, we'd have dinner, he'd correct his homework and we'd watch a little television before he went to bed. I'd sit in my bedroom and grade papers, then fall asleep exhausted. I considered quitting at *Gay Chicago*, but I loved the work, and I was making good money there. Ralph and Dan were always very generous when it came to my salary.

We got used to the schedule, though Adam occasionally screwed it up by missing his school bus. Then I'd get a call at work, and he'd have to go to the neighborhood school, but he seemed to get along with the kids there, and he knew many of them from attending the local Boy's Club. Still, it was clear our living situation had to change. I started looking for a house or townhouse. I didn't have any equity in the condo. It was the days of "$250 down, no credit check!" I did have savings. It was supposed to be my money for the summer – teachers only got paid during the school year in those days. But if I got a summer job, I could use it for a down payment. I quickly found out my budget wouldn't go far if I wanted to be in a good neighborhood. Now that I had Adam, a sketchy up and coming neighborhood wasn't an option. I ended up finding an abandoned house in Andersonville, formerly Chicago's Swedish neighborhood.

Andersonville is now very trendy, but in the mid-1980s it was pretty desolate. Not dangerous, but certainly not someplace most people thought of as a popular neighborhood for gay people. Karen Triner-Ross, the typesetter at *Gay Chicago,* mentioned that her husband was a handyman. I asked him if he could help make the house livable. He agreed to defer payment until I got it fixed up and could refinance. All set! I rented out my condo. Then Michael backed out of the deal. I had nowhere to go. The house was filthy and uninhabitable, and my tenant had already moved into my condo.

My parents had a huge five-bedroom house, and only my youngest brother lived at home. I asked them if Adam and I could stay with them, paying them rent for a month or so, while I made my house habitable. They agreed and even though I was working a full-time job and rehabbing the house on my own, I still managed to help around my parent's house, mowing the lawn, etc. Two weeks into the arrangement, my youngest sister called home. She was leaving her husband and moving back from California. She wanted to stay with my parents as well. Adam and I were given 24 hours-notice; we were booted out. This was typical behavior for my parents.

With my plans out the window, I scrambled. A friend from the Parents Group had a roommate who was working in Provincetown for the summer. He liked kids and let me rent the room. He knew Adam and didn't mind him hanging out while I was at work. Every day I was up at the crack of dawn and worked the breakfast shift at my friend's restaurant. By early afternoon, I would pick up Adam, we'd grab some lunch and head up to the house where we'd work until about ten.

The windows were rattling in their frames, the plaster was crumbling, and the wall-to-wall carpeting was pee-soaked and stapled every four inches. After cleaning and repairing what we could, Adam and I would be filthy dirty as we'd board the bus back to my friend's apartment. On weekends, when my ex-wife took Adam, I worked from 7:00 in the morning until 10:00 at night. Rehabbing that house was back-breaking labor, during one of the hottest summers on record. I had little in the way of home repair skills and even less money. It was just Adam and me hauling out garbage, pulling up carpeting and doing what we could. I applied for a dozen credit cards and charged all the work that I couldn't do; plumbing, electrical and refinishing what turned out to be gorgeous wide-plank wooden floors. I made minimum payments on the credit cards (at 18 to 24% interest) until everything was done. After the repairs, which included installing a kitchen because there hadn't been one, I refinanced the house and paid off all the credit cards. I even had enough money left to install a second bathroom and reroute the stairway to the second floor. I got lucky. At that time interest rates kept dropping, so each time I refinanced my payments dropped. Within a year, Adam and I had a beautiful home.

Jeff McCourt called me about a year after I bought my house and asked if he could come over, as he had a housewarming present for me. I was surprised; we weren't close friends. We were cordial when we ran into each other at events, but that was it. I supposed he was lonely, so I agreed, and set up a time when Adam would be at his mother's house. I didn't want to take a chance on Jeff's erratic behavior.

Jeff showed up with a beautiful oriental rug. It was an unusual housewarming gift. I assumed it was given to him and he was regifting it. We sat in my living room. He sipped a scotch – which he brought with him. I had a glass of wine. It was an uncomfortable visit. Then the real reason for his visit came out. He wanted me to leave *Gay Chicago* and work for him at *Windy City Times*. I could be the features editor. I was flattered and shocked. *Gay Chicago* was a fun bar guide and on the verge of becoming something more, but *Windy City Times* was one of the most highly regarded gay newspapers in the country. I was hesitant. I'd heard horror stories of how Jeff would throw tantrums in the *Windy City Times* offices. The fact that he was using cocaine only added to his erratic personality. It got to the point where his office was on one floor, and the rest of the staff was on another.

Ralph might get a little snarky when he was drunk – which was often, though never at the office. Dan, on the other hand got nicer when he drank. Alcohol was a problem at *Gay Chicago*, but not to the extent that drugs were with Jeff (and a few others) at *Windy City Times*. Then there was the issue of Adam. *Windy City Times*' offices weren't anywhere near his school. How would I arrange for after-school care for him? He was in 7$^{th}$ grade now, but I didn't feel comfortable leaving him on his own.

I told Jeff I was flattered, but I was happy at *Gay Chicago*. Jeff shrugged and said that if I ever wanted to "jump the fence" I was welcome. We then went bar hopping, until Jeff met up with some folks I assumed were drug suppliers. I was invited along but begged off and went home, alone, as usual.

# CHAPTER 16

\* \* \*

Not only was my gossip column the most popular column in the magazine, but it was also now running two to three pages. For most of our readers, it was the first column they turned to. Again, much of it was taken from press releases: people hired at the bars and clubs, not-for-profit agencies serving the community, new businesses opening, community events and the like. I mixed that with bar and club events, along with tips I received via my *Gay Chicago* voicemail. The column got me invited to many events in the community, including black-tie galas. I developed friendships with some of the people at these agencies and businesses. I wasn't kidding myself; I knew they were making sure their events or news were covered, but a few friendships developed as well. It was also how I met my first LTR (long-term relationship, remember?)

One day I was chatting with folks after a performance by the Chicago Gay Men's Chorus when I saw a dark, Mediterranean-looking man with striking blue eyes and a sparkling smile. I'd already noticed him singing on stage during the performance. Then at the after-party, I approached him. After years of standing on the sidelines, waiting for men to approach me, I decided to take the initiative. I was a brazen flirt, and it often worked. I walked up to the man I'd been admiring and chatted him up. While we didn't go home together that night, we made a date. The next week after a movie and a romantic dinner, we went back to his place and started to make out. After about 20 minutes we both realized that neither of us was into it. We stopped, hung out chatting for a while, and then parted. His name was Danny Kopelson and he and I remained cordial, although we didn't socialize together. Then I ran into Danny at a community event. He mentioned he was having a birthday party and invited me. I was fairly certain it was only so his name would appear in my column, but I took down the information. On the day of the party, Adam was at his mother's house for the weekend, and I was alone. I remembered Danny's invitation and decided to go. I still didn't have a car, so I walked from my house in Andersonville to Sheridan Road to catch a bus to his place on Cornelia near Lake Shore Drive.

Andersonville was a quiet neighborhood back then, but the area between Broadway and Sheridan was rough. As I was walking through, I was approached by a large imposing man. I was carrying a bottle of wine for the party, and he tried to grab it from me. I was afraid I was going to be mugged, so I smashed the bottle against the wall and held it in front of me as a weapon. The guy ran away. Frightened, no doubt, by my crazy behavior. My bipolar tendencies were reasonably controlled by my medication, but the fear and rush of adrenalin made me manic. I was shaking, and my heart was pounding, when I got to Danny's apartment. I'm sure my entrance caused quite a stir, but after a shot or two, I calmed down.

When I entered the living room where most of the party guests were located, I locked eyes with a man. I stopped suddenly. It was like the movie cliché where everything goes soft focus, and the two people drift together, unaware of everyone around them, like Maria and Tony in *West Side Story*. Cliché or not, that's how it felt the first time I saw Chuck Erhardt. I'd dated a few people over the years, but no one who made my heart flutter as much as my first love, Chris Carlson.

Chuck was the same type, medium height and blond with a baby face. But that's where the similarities ended. Chuck was sturdy and grounded, whereas Chris had been flighty. I fell in love right there. For once, the feelings were returned. We spent the entire evening huddled in a corner talking. It turned out that he was Danny's best friend. He came home with me that night, and we spent the night making love. He had to work the next day but wanted to meet that night. I readily agreed. We were an instant couple. I felt so sure of the relationship, I did something I'd never done before, I introduced him to Adam.

A month or so later he told me his lease was up and he was moving to a new apartment. On an impulse I asked him to move in with us. We were a perfect match. He grounded me, was a homebody, and he and Adam got along well. After being alone for so many years, it was good to have someone to share a life with. Although, after being alone for so long I was also set in my way of parenting. More than once, we clashed over how to discipline Adam when he was disrespectful or violated house rules.

Chuck was good to me and easy to be with. He was handy around the house. He landscaped our yard, turning it into a showplace. We went away for a romantic weekend in Saugatuck, Michigan. We stayed at a B&B, drank wine while we sat in a hot tub, and walked along the beach. He even loved the show tune sing-along at a bar called Sidetrack, as I did. That year my birthday fell on a Monday. He surprised me at show tune night at Sidetrack with a big cake. That birthday was magical, my first with a partner. We both had too much to drink, stumbled into a taxi, went home, and made love.

There were many nights like that. I soon realized that Chuck was a heavy drinker, at least by my standards. I usually drank one or two white wine spritzers when I went out – very big in the '70s and '80s. It would never occur to me to pour a drink when I was at home. Neither of my parents were big drinkers. I was now drinking gin to keep up with Chuck. I found myself getting drunk a lot, so I stopped. Chuck didn't. When he was at home, he drank beer, when we went out, gin. The one short relationship I'd had before Chuck was a mean drunk. But Chuck never became mean. He grew maudlin when he drank beer, romantic on gin. So, my guard was down.

What I wasn't ready for was his disappearing act. If we had a disagreement, he'd storm out of the house and not return for days. When he came back, he was full of regret, and we'd reconcile. After almost a year together, we had a disagreement and he disappeared again, this time for three days. I called Danny, frantic to see if he'd heard from Chuck. He hadn't. When Chuck staggered back into the house, his pants were unzipped and open. Thank goodness Adam wasn't there at the time. I put him to bed, told Danny that Chuck was safe and that I was going to have a serious talk with him.

The next day when Chuck arrived home from work, I confronted him. What I didn't know is that Danny had talked to him about his drinking that same day. I guess he thought we coordinated our efforts and were attacking him. He blew up, packed some of his things, and walked out. The fight may have been about the drinking, but there were other issues, my lack of flexibility when it came to disciplining Adam, and lack of trust, in general. I knew it was the end; there was no coming back from this. He came home when I was at work and removed the rest of his clothing. He called one day, but only to make arrangements for picking up his final things. He arrived with a friend to help him. Chuck had done so much around the house, I tried to offer him money; I felt I owed him that. He refused, but he did try to take a wooden toilet seat he'd installed in our bathroom. That's what we ended up fighting over. I literally yanked it out of his arms, before slamming the door in his face.

Within a few months, Chuck quit his job at the florist around the corner from our house and disappeared from the community. Neither Danny nor I ever heard from him again. However, out of that relationship, I got custody of Danny, who became and remained one of my closest friends, and started what turned out to be one of Chicago's most-enduring fundraising events.

### Night of 100 Drag Queens: Sidetrack, Show Tunes, and Chicago's Longest Running Charitable Fundraiser:

March 16, 1987 wasn't a significant birthday for me, I was turning 34 – not a milestone. But since it fell on a Monday, Chuck and I decided to celebrate it at my favorite bar, Sidetrack. As I said, I wasn't the bar type before I came out, but working at *Gay Chicago* required going to events. It wasn't so difficult now that I knew a few people in the community. Bars traditionally served as a town center for the LGBTQ community, so I became more comfortable going to them. I wasn't much of a drinker, so I went to socialize, meet men, be entertained, or sometimes all three. I liked Sidetrack because Monday night was show tune video night. To pick up business on slow Monday nights, Pepin Pena and Art Johnston, the owners of Sidetrack, played all show tune music videos. My friend Lauren Cowling and I went out to dinner on Monday nights, then headed over to Sidetrack. Back then, I could go out on week nights, stay at the bar until closing, and get up in time to get Adam to school and me to work – Adam was 13 now, old enough to spend the evening by himself. Chuck threw a show tune-themed birthday party. He ordered a huge cake and bought a case of champagne from the bar and invited everyone I knew with the caveat – no gifts. I really didn't need anything, except materials to rehab my house and I knew no one was going to gift wrap a piece of drywall. So, on the invitation he asked that instead of gifts or a card, a donation be made to the Gay Parents' Group. The night of the party, we showed up at Sidetrack, staked out the corner Arthur and Pepe had set out for us, put a donation jar on the bar, and just hung out. Dozens of friends came by. Almost every member of the parents' group, a couple of straight co-workers from my school and some old friends from high school stopped in. Many of the community's leaders and even just folks I didn't know who read my column stopped by as well. In fact, there were so many people, I had to order another case of champagne about two hours into the party. I was overwhelmed. The jar of cash on the bar was stuffed full. At one point there was a pause in the music. I thought they wanted me to make a speech, but suddenly space in the middle of the bar was cleared, beer cases were dragged out, and a piece of plywood was balanced on top of them. Then two drag queens got up on the makeshift stage and performed. The bar had arranged the performance as a treat for me. The drag queens were Paula Sinclaire and Vikki Spykke. I was delighted. It was the best birthday I ever had. I raised more than $500 for the parents' group.

The next year, even though Chuck and I had broken up, I did the same thing. The bar put together an even bigger show, with some of the bartenders getting up and doing numbers in drag. This was a real treat because, unlike some gay bars, there were seldom drag shows at Sidetrack. In fact, except for Halloween, my birthday was it.

Eventually, show tune Monday became so popular that Sidetrack moved the event to Sunday afternoons. When that happened, my birthday parties moved to Sunday. I rented out the bar for a couple of hours before they opened on Sunday afternoon and I prepared a themed buffet. One year it was trailer trash with spam and macaroni and cheese on the buffet. Folks ate it all! I invited everyone I knew. The donations to charity grew bigger, as did the drag shows. It got to a point where the bar built a stage just for the party.

Arthur, Pepe and their manager and eventual business partner Chuck Hyde, got liquor companies to underwrite the party, boosting the amount we donated to the Gay & Lesbian Parents' Group. The party became a highly anticipated event, and about the third or fourth year I said to Chuck, "I think we should give the party a name."

I came up with "Night of 100 Drag Queens," making fun of an annual television special "Night of 100 Stars." Our show had grown, but we still didn't have 100 drag queens performing. However, it was in keeping with my writing style of making everything seem grandiose to the point of ridiculousness. Chuck liked the idea, got even more underwriting and that year we were able to raise more than $5,000 for the Gay & Lesbian Parent's Group International.

After doing that for five years for a variety of charities, we got hit with a severe storm – mid-March in Chicago is still the dead of winter. It was hard enough walking through the snow, much less in heels. So, we decided to move the party to the week before Halloween. Night of 100 Drag Queens continued through 2017 as a benefit for Equality Illinois and at its peak, featured two nights of shows and two stages just to accommodate the crowds.

There have been many notable performances, on and off stage through the years. During the early years, we used a nearby beauty shop as a dressing room. One time, a drunk guy wandered in and started causing trouble. Another performer and I grabbed him and tossed him out the door. Half an hour later, the cops showed up, the guy wanted to file a complaint. So, there I am standing in a bustier, pantyhose, and heels, explaining to the cop what happened. They eventually arrested the guy for disorderly conduct.

On stage, two performances stand out. One was community leader Victor Salvo making his debut in drag, looking exactly like Barbra Streisand in *Funny Girl*. For the *Don't Rain on My Parade* number he entered with suitcases. For the finale on the boat, he reached into his suitcase and pulled out the railing Barbra stands in front of. The audience went wild. Another event was not as noticeable to the audience, but we had a deaf man do drag. I don't know how he was able to lip-sync, but it was a beautiful moment for me.

The event, over the years, raised more than one million dollars for charity and it all started with a sheet cake and a case of cheap champagne.

# CHAPTER 17

## ✳ ✳ ✳

In June of 1987, just before Chuck and I broke up, I got a message on my voicemail telling me that Chuck Renslow, who owned a building in Uptown which housed Man's Country, a gay bathhouse, planned on converting part of the building into a nightclub. It made sense. Attendance at bathhouses was down because of the AIDS crisis. Renslow and his long-time friend, Eddie Dugan, were converting the bathhouse's old performance hall into a dance club and planned to call it Bistro Too. Eddie Dugan was the face of Dugan's Bistro, Chicago's most popular disco in the 1970s. I called Renslow's office to confirm the story. I was given a tour of the building while the conversion was in progress. It was a big scoop and the lead item in my column the next week.

I got lots of leaked information via my voicemail. I would always delete the message as soon as I took down the information so that anyone who might be able to identify the voice couldn't listen to it. Most people in the community knew I was discreet, which is why I got so many scoops over the years. The way to survive as a gossip columnist is to know when to keep your mouth shut! I got another big scoop via my voicemail soon after that. Somebody at *Windy City Times* witnessed a big blow out between Tracy Baim and Jeff McCourt after which she walked out. I was the first to report that Baim left *Windy City Times*, the same week her name was out of the masthead. No official announcement had been made. The "little bird" who left me a voicemail told me Tracy was out, and the ubiquitous Albert "Bill" Williams was replacing her. What they didn't mention, but I found out, was that *Windy City Times'* advertising manager, Jill Burgin, left with her. Something about that was suspicious. Sure enough, on June 6, just two weeks later, Tracy Baim put out her own publication, *Chicago Outlines.* Jeff's staff walked out on him, just as he had done to Renslow a couple of years earlier.

What's more, Tracy and Jill had the advertising contacts. In various interviews, Baim has said she tried to get enough investors together to buy out McCourt. Anyone with the slightest understanding of Jeff knows that *Windy City Times* was his "baby." He would no more relinquish control of the publication than cut off a limb. Baim had to know that. There was no way she could plan a buy-out, her only option was to go out on her own, giving Chicago three gay weeklies.

The preponderance of gay publications shouldn't have been a shock to anyone. Chicago has always been a newspaper town. In print journalism's heyday, the city supported six daily newspapers as well as two niche publications serving the Jewish and Black communities and numerous-foreign language weeklies. Jeff was, in fact, partially to blame for his competition. He had proven to mainstream advertisers that there was a gay market, and now they were willing to advertise in the gay press.

Jeff, writing as Mimi O'Shea in the "Dirt" gossip column spewed venom at Tracy Baim. Mimi printed a list of movies Baim was supposedly watching, *Bill of Divorcement, Mutiny on the Bounty* and *The Year of Living Dangerously.* All veiled references to what he saw as her betrayal. Try as he might to disparage her, one thing Baim had going for her was her dedication to Chicago's LGBTQ press. Everyone respected her commitment and determination, even if they disagreed with her personally. Jeff also made mention of yet another publication for Chicago's gay community. The four-color, glossy monthly was to be titled *Rage.* The magazine finally debuted in October of that year, listing Bill Brownell as publisher. It lasted one issue.

# Tracy Baim

She has labored untiringly since 1984 as publisher, reporter, editor, columnist, and photographer in offering a voice to all segments of the community. In 2000, her company bought the weekly Windy City Times and merged her weekly Outlines into it. She also publishes the weekly Nightspots, plus BLACKlines, En La Vida, and the OUT!Resource Guide, besides airing Windy City Radio. In addition, she helped to found and has co-chaired the Chicago Gay and Lesbian Chamber of Commerce.

Tracy Baim, a 31-year-old native of Chicago, has made a tremendous impact during her ten-year career in the gay and lesbian press in Chicago. She has contributed her untiring efforts as publisher, journalist, editor, and photographer in providing a voice to all segments of our community. Currently, the publisher and managing editor of Lambda Publications, which produces Blacklines, Nightlines, Outlines, and the OUT! Resource Guide, Baim has written over 2,500 articles, columns, and editorials. Each of these publications provides a venue highlighting not only national and local news of immediate importance to the gay and lesbian community but also focusing attention on the diversity and depth of our cultural achievements.

Baim received a degree in journalism from Drake University in 1984. Upon graduating, she took a job as editorial assistant at GayLife, becoming managing editor there a year later. In the fall of 1985, she helped to found Windy City Times, and in 1987 she was the founding publisher and managing editor of Outlines. During that time, she has covered thousands of events, from bar parties and sports tournaments to black-tie benefits.

It is the support of her coworkers, family, and friends, along with the backing of the community in general, which has allowed Baim to maintain her 70+-hour-a-week schedule for ten years. With a keen eye for news and her ever-faithful camera, she chronicles our day-to-day lives.

She has won considerable recognition for her work. She was a finalist for editorial writing in the 1993 and 1994 Peter Lisagor Chicago Journalism Awards. She has been recognized by NOW: Chicago Chapter, Dignity, and the 1987 and 1993 Marches on Washington. She was named MVP of Chicago's 1993-94 indoor soccer season and has been honored as a Lee K. Bubblehead. Baim was a recipient of the 1994 Chicago Torch Award presented by the Human Rights Campaign Fund.

While speaking at Valparaiso University's Martin Luther King Day celebration, Baim stated, "What I really want is for all gays and lesbians to accept themselves. I would like for the internal homophobia to stop, for the self-destructive behavior and the suicide to end. All we seek from society is the right to live peacefully, without violence and discrimination based on our sexual orientation. Our future depends on making sure everyone is included."

A strong advocate of human rights, Baim continues her vocal battle against racism, sexism, and homophobia. Editorials such as her award-winning "Go Home, Faggots" provide an opportunity to reflect on the current state of our lives and on possibilities for the future. She holds up a mirror to the society in which we live and is not afraid to spotlight its blemishes.

Source: The Chicago LGBT Hall of Fame website at
glhalloffame.org
Baim was inducted in 2004

# CHAPTER 18

\* \* \*

I t was time for a change at *Gay Chicago*. After starting in Ralph
Gernhardt's apartment in Old Town, he and Dan Di Leo rented offices,
sharing a storefront with an art gallery. That's where Adam would go after
school each day. That was fine when there were six of us working on the
magazine, but additional advertisers meant extra ad salespeople, and they
needed space for desks. It was time to move again. Ralph and Dan found office
space on the second floor of a parking garage on Broadway, south of Belmont.
The move put the office right in the heart of the gay community. It was a big
step up, and when we moved in that summer, there was quite a celebration.
Now Adam took the school bus to *Gay Chicago*'s office, when he didn't have
kung fu practice or some other after-school activity.

That fall was a busy time. Chicago was about to have its first big-ticket
AIDS fundraising event, "A Show of Concern" with Angela Lansbury as emcee
and appearances by Leslie Uggams, Jerry Herman, Chita Rivera, Oprah
Winfrey, Sandy Duncan, and Colleen Dewhurst. The papers were also filled
with information on the first major demonstration in Washington D.C. by the
gay and lesbian community. Local contingents were working as part of a
nationwide network for the first time. If the AIDS crisis decimated our
community, it also brought us together to fight a common enemy. For all the

talk that AIDS was not a "gay" disease, it was the gay and lesbian community that fought the hardest, raised the most funds and supported those impacted by the disease.

I'd lost only a few close friends to AIDS at that point, but we all viewed the disease as a death sentence, and we were all scared shitless. That is why I attended the October 11 March on Washington in 1987. I felt that everyone had to show up to let the world – and the U.S. government – know that the gay and lesbian community was a force to be reckoned with. What I didn't expect was the emotional impact of being in a city where gays and lesbians were in the majority (at least for that weekend). In 1987, the population of Washington D.C. was a little over 600,000. Knowing that traffic would be a nightmare, many residents left the city for the weekend and tourists postponed their visits. Police estimates for the size of the crowd, at its peak, was more than half a million. If we weren't officially in the majority, we were undoubtedly the majority of the people out and about that weekend. I remember coming down the long escalator at DuPont Circle. A man in a booming baritone belted out "Oh what a beautiful morning..." by the third line of the song, the entire crowd were singing together. My heart fluttered – as it does writing about it now – and I thought, "This is what Jews must feel like when they go to Israel for the first time." I was among my people. I was home.

Another aspect of the October '87 March on Washington for me was developing a deeper relationship with *Gay Chicago*'s political cartoonist, Danny Sotomayor. We just happened to run into each other on the street and overcome with the emotion of the moment, hugged. We spent that afternoon exploring Washington together, parted at some point, and went our separate ways. From that day forward, whenever he'd drop off his political cartoons, he'd stop by my desk and say hello. At least until he and Ralph Paul Gernhardt had a disagreement about one of Danny's cartoons.

The magazine's co-publishers Ralph Paul Gernhardt and Dan Di Leo had different views on Danny's work. Gernhardt felt that *Gay Chicago*, as an entertainment guide, shouldn't be running editorial cartoons. Di Leo, a journalist, felt otherwise and was Sotomayor's main supporter. In 1990, after a particularly vehement exchange with the mayor, Sotomayor submitted a cartoon, as he did every week. The cartoon depicted a ship as a metaphor for City Hall, with the Mayor Richard M. Daley's press secretary Avis LaVelle shoving a paper bag down over the mayor's head, while his special assistant, Nancy Reiff, nudged Jon Simmons, the mayor's liaison to the gay and lesbian community, off a plank.

Gernhardt, a staunch Daley supporter, immediately rejected the cartoon. He placed it in a cabinet behind his desk. Dan Di Leo felt the cartoon had merit, but acquiesced to Ralph, in support of Reiff. At the time Di Leo was also battling complications from HIV infection.

Sotomayor used the cartoon on political fliers, one of which was faxed to the mayor's office. Gernhardt was furious. He felt that Sotomayor had betrayed him. Di Leo, who might have defended Sotomayor, as he had in the past, was now hospitalized and died a few days later, on Thanksgiving. Gernhardt removed Sotomayor's name from *Gay Chicago*'s masthead the next issue and told Sotomayor he was fired the following week.

Sotomayor's work started appearing in *Windy City Times* within a week and his cartoons ran there until his death a few years later, in November of 1992.

There was more going on in the battle over Danny's cartoon than most people knew. Simmons was a well-liked community member, a hold-over from the Washington administration. He was being edged out by Nancy Reiff, who was more polarizing. She'd been a bar manager and had also worked at *Gay Chicago*. Reiff and Gernhardt were close. Gernhardt might also have been gun-shy after *Gay Chicago* ran a cover illustration of former Mayor Harold Washington holding Chicago on a tray. While the intention was not to demean the mayor, many saw the image as racist – although, Mayor Washington himself thought it was funny. Also, Gerhardt was dealing with the grief of losing his best friend and business partner to AIDS.

Danny was rightfully angry. I thought then, and still believe now, that Ralph was wrong. I think his decision was fueled by grief. Ralph never asked my opinion on the subject, and Danny's work didn't have anything to do with me or my section of the magazine. I later discovered Danny was furious with me, blaming me for the entire fiasco. I think he thought I had more influence over Ralph than I did. Danny never spoke to me again. He wouldn't even let me explain my point of view. When he died a few years later, I mourned the loss of a talented man, but one who I never got to know as much as I would have liked to.

# Daniel Sotomayor

Daniel Sotomayor was born on August 30, 1958. He grew up in the Humboldt Park area of Chicago, a troubled youth of Mexican and Puerto Rican descent. He attended Prosser High School, studied acting at the Center Theatre, attended the American Academy of Art and graduated from Columbia College with a degree in graphic arts. He began to pursue a career in acting and graphic design.

Daniel's HIV seroconversion and sudden diagnosis with AIDS in 1988 shattered his personal and professional aspirations, awakening in him the activist who changed forever the standard by which our community leaders are judged.

After joining ACTUP/CHICAGO, Daniel proceeded through sheer force of will to propel that organization to its highest effective visibility. Daniel became widely known for his public confrontations with Mayor Richard M. Daley to bring attention to the AIDS crisis, the Chicago Health Department's responsibility to implement the City's AIDS Strategic Plan and inadequate education, prevention, and media programs.

Daniel also established himself as the first nationally syndicated, openly gay political cartoonist. During his brief but brilliant three-year career, he created over two hundred scathing, and often humorous, cartoons illustrating his anger with AIDS, with government inaction, with the insurance industry, the health care system, pharmaceutical companies, and, frequently, with AIDS activists themselves.

Daniel has left his indelible mark on the AIDS movement, on our community's awakening as a political force, on the minds of "leaders" who have had reason to fear his unblinking honesty, and on the hearts of those who came to know the human being behind the headlines. Daniel's relentless pursuit of the truth helped him to live his life with a consistency of ethic that most of us can only aspire towards. In doing so, he changed forever our definition of "leader."

He was an openly gay, nationally syndicated political cartoonist and prominent Chicago AIDS activist. He died of AIDS complications on February 5, 1992.

Source: The Chicago LGBT Hall of Fame website at
glhalloffame.org
Sotomayor was inducted in 1992, deceased 1992

*The author and his son as a toddler.*

*Poster for the musical, "Spin Cycle."*

*Author (right) with "Spin Cycle" composer Frank DePaul (left)..*

*Publicity still from "Spin Cycle" with Scott Mullen (left), Sandy Jamieson (center), and Diane Brown (right).*

*Family portrait of author (right), his son Adam (center) and Chuck E. (left)*

*Author with the She Devils at "Cruising for a Dreamboat."*

*Front cover of "Gay Chicago" announcing the first installment of "Death on the Rocks."*

*Front cover of "Gay Chicago" announcing the first After Dark Awards.*

*Author (left, middle row) with Cruising for a Dreamboat "bachelors."*

*Front cover of "Gay Chicago" promoting "Making a Commitment to Love."*

*Author getting ready for a special appearance at "Night of 100 Drag Queens."*

*The author (right) and son, Adam as a young man (left).*

*"Wedding" in Washington D.C, April 1993. The author's husband Gregg (center, bottom row) and the author, to his right.*

*The author (left) and his husband Gregg Schapiro (right).*

*Author receiving the Chicago LGBT Hall of Fame award from Chicago Mayor, Richard M. Daley.*

*The author today r (center), his son Adam (left) and husband Gregg Shapiro (right)*

# CHAPTER 19

## ✱ ✱ ✱

Thanksgiving weekend of 1987, Mayor Harold Washington died of a heart attack. It sent shockwaves through Chicago's Gay and Lesbian community. While the previous mayor, Jane Byrne, may have talked about supporting the gay community she never did anything other than to issue a Mayoral Proclamation for Pride. Washington opened the doors of City Hall to the LGBTQ community, as well as other communities not part of Chicago's machine politics. Mayor Washington appointed a liaison to the Gay and Lesbian community. Granted, it was a straight, white woman, but Kit Duffy embraced the job and advocated for our cause. After a while, everyone assumed she was a lesbian and accepted her as one of our own. Washington eventually moved Duffy to a more senior role in his administration, replacing her with an openly gay man, Jon Simmons. Soon after Washington's death, Duffy resigned but remained an active ally of the community. Simmons stayed on in his role through the transitional administrations. Years later, he was murdered while on vacation in California.

# Katherine "Kit" Duffy

Katherine (Kit) Duffy, 64, for her advocacy for LGBT rights, including her 1984 appointment by Mayor Harold Washington as the first mayoral liaison to Chicago's LGBT communities and her role in securing the 1988 passage of an ordinance barring discrimination against gays and lesbians in Chicago.

Kit Duffy has earned a place as a Friend of the Community in the Chicago Gay and Lesbian Hall of Fame. Born in Hagerstown, Maryland, in 1944, she has resided in Chicago since 1964. In February 1984, she was appointed by then-Mayor Harold Washington as his liaison to Chicago's gay and lesbian communities. This was the first such appointment in Chicago history.

One of her first actions as liaison was to arrange an open-ended meeting between city department heads and a wide-ranging group of lesbian and gay activists and leaders. "That was very symbolic of what Harold was trying to do for the whole community," Duffy recalled in 2007, emphasizing that Washington was determined to give everyone equal access to city services and power. It was a heady era, as Washington fought to make Chicago's government more responsive to residents' desires and concerns.

"The one thing that really struck me throughout the time that I served as liaison to the community was the way that process paralleled what Harold was trying to do for the entire city. It was certainly time for that change," she continued. "We were flying blind, but with a complete commitment to fairness."

During her tenure as mayoral liaison, Duffy worked tirelessly to foster a sense of political empowerment throughout Chicago's lesbian and gay communities. In 1985, she convened Mayor Washington's Committee on Gay and Lesbian Issues, the precursor to today's Advisory Council on Lesbian, Gay, Bisexual and Transgender Issues. Also, in 1985, she became the first executive director of the newly-formed AIDS Foundation of Chicago.

After Washington's untimely death in November 1987, Duffy remained a vocal advocate for equal rights and assisted a campaign, which had begun in 1973 and succeeded in 1988, to secure passage of a historic ordinance banning discrimination against gays and lesbians in employment, housing, and public accommodations. In 1991, Duffy was one of the co-founders of the Illinois Federation for Human Rights (forerunner of today's Equality Illinois), along with Jon-Henri Damski, Rick Garcia, Lana Hostetler, and Art Johnston. She remains an ardent advocate for LGBT rights.

Source: The Chicago LGBT Hall of Fame website at glhalloffame.org
Duffy was inducted in 2008, deceased 2015

## Jon A. Simmons

Jon Simmons (1955-1994), a city government liaison to LGBT Chicagoans under three mayors. Before being appointed by Mayor Eugene Sawyer in 1988, he had been Joseph Holmes Dance Theatre's executive director and a freelance writer and researcher. He was found murdered in Beverly Hills, Calif., while on a 1994 vacation.

Jon A. Simmons described himself as a "Gay Everyman," but his accomplishments and civic dedication were nothing short of extraordinary.

He was born February 15, 1955, in Pittsburgh, Pennsylvania. The resident of Chicago's Lakeview neighborhood received his bachelor's degree in English and writing from Columbia College in 1983 and served on the Illinois State Scholarship Commission as a student member from 1983 to 1985. From 1985 to 1988 he was executive director of Chicago's Joseph Holmes Dance Theatre. He was also a freelance writer for *Windy City Times*.

Simmons went on to have an enduring influence on the city's LGBT communities by building ties between them and a succession of Chicago mayors: Harold Washington, Eugene Sawyer, and Richard M. Daley. In 1985, he was tapped by Mayor Washington to serve on his groundbreaking Committee on Gay and Lesbian Issues and was subsequently elected to chair the committee. In 1988, after Mayor Sawyer had succeeded

Washington in 1987, the new mayor named Simmons as his coordinator for gay and lesbian issues.

The influence that Simmons developed became even greater during the early years of the Richard M. Daley administration. Two years after his 1989 election, Mayor Daley reorganized the Commission on Human Relations, creating the Advisory Council on Gay and Lesbian Issues, and the mayor picked Simmons to serve as its director. The advisory council sponsored, among other things, the Chicago Gay and Lesbian Hall of Fame, which was also created in 1991.

Simmons's earlier role had helped to lay a foundation, by providing a link between LGBT Chicagoans and the mayor's office, which aided the eventual passage of the historic 1988 measure popularly called the Human Rights Ordinance. The ordinance added sexual orientation to the categories of discrimination explicitly prohibited by city law.

He stepped down from his advisory council post in 1991 to pursue a law degree at IIT Chicago-Kent College of Law. By mid-1994, the 39-year-old had graduated and was preparing to take the Illinois bar examination, but first he decided to take a well-earned vacation. On the night of October 1, 1994, while spending a few days in Los Angeles, where he had been joined by his San Francisco brother before continuing on an intended visit to Hawaii, Simmons was shot to death during a night out. His body was found early the next morning in a Beverly Hills alley. His murder remains unsolved.

Chicago government subsequently honored Simmons with a commemorative street designation. Signs reading "Honorary Jon Simmons Parade" mark each end of West Cornelia Avenue between North Halsted Street and North Broadway in recognition of his legacy.

Source: The Chicago LGBT Hall of Fame website at
glhalloffame.org
Simmons was inducted in 2011, deceased 1994

Mayor Harold Washington's sudden death put the city's Democratic machine into overdrive trying to disassemble Washington's new coalition of minority groups. The machine had battled Washington with racism, only occasionally thinly veiled, much as the Republicans did during Barack Obama's presidency. There was a power struggle immediately after Washington's death. Eugene Sawyer, a black city council member who managed to work with both the Democratic machine and Washington's independents, was appointed interim mayor.

*Windy City Times* gained even more stature as both sides of the struggle realized they needed the gay vote to take back power. McCourt used that opportunity to help him overcome Tracy Baim's departure. While Baim bad-mouthed McCourt all over town, she couldn't argue with his success at marketing the paper or its stature in the community. Although she could never have toppled *Windy City Times*, if it wasn't for the timing, she could have done a lot more damage.

I chatted with Jeff when he stopped in the *Gay Chicago* office during the annual holiday party. In addition to being a party for the staff, Ralph also invited advertisers and community leaders. *Gay Chicago* remained friendly with *Windy City Times*, unlike Tracy and *Outlines*. Part of that animosity was that Ralph resented Tracy's feminism. Some of the most sexist men could be found in the gay community. But it was also because Tracy, realizing that *Outlines* wasn't going to overtake *Windy City*, went after *Gay Chicago*'s advertisers. She tried to position her publication as an alternative to both of us.

However, rightly or wrongly, *Outlines* was viewed as a "lesbian" publication and, consequently, many men's bars wouldn't advertise. Even though our advertisers wouldn't leave us for Outlines, Ralph resented Tracy for trying to poach them. He didn't see the irony in that our advertising reps were always trying to "steal" her advertisers – it's just the nature of the business.

Jeff and I chatted in a corner during the party, he again tried to convince me that I should leave *Gay Chicago*. I mentioned my hesitation about working with Bill Williams, whose attitude just irked me. Jeff intimated that Bill was just filling in temporarily and that he had someone lined up to replace him after the first of the year, someone that would increase *Windy City Times*' journalistic reputation.

In late January, Mark Shoofs took over as editor. He was Yale-educated and already establishing a reputation as a top-notch journalist and AIDS activist. Mark, who would later go on to write for *The Wall Street Journal* and *The Village Voice* brought *Windy City Times* national recognition when he won a Peter Lisagor Award. He would later go on to win a Pulitzer Prize in 2000 for his series in *The Village Voice* on AIDS in Africa. He was also among a group of journalists nominated as Pulitzer finalists for a series on Medicare fraud in 2011. He has since moved into on-line media working for ProPublica and BuzzFeed.

*Outlines* continued struggling to gain its footing. It didn't help that *Windy City Times* was offering advertisers bargain rates to keep them exclusive. By the beginning of 1988 McCourt had won over so many advertisers that Baim had no choice but to change her plans. She announced that the publication would become a tabloid, publishing monthly. The new format debuted on February 11. The monthly format and new design allowed *Outlines* to survive. Still, it was never real competition for either *Windy City Times* or *Gay Chicago,* as was evidenced in the Pride issues of 1988. *Windy City Times* published three sections totaling 156 pages, *Gay Chicago* moved to a larger 9"x12" format (from its former pocket-sized guide), with a full-color cover. The magazine contained the maximum number of pages (112) that its binding process allowed and was actually turning away advertisers. Meanwhile, *Outlines'* 86-page issue contained a vast number of free ads given to not-for-profits. The remaining ads were offered at a discounted rate in order to pad the issue.

# CHAPTER 20

Ralph had been hesitant to change from the pocket-sized digest format he'd used since the first edition of *Gay Chicago*. However, the reaction to the larger format used for the 1988 Pride issue was mostly positive. A few weeks after Pride, Ralph approached me at my desk and asked me to step into the conference room. I was worried that one of the snarky comments in my gossip column was about to get me fired. I was still on shaky ground after a major error. I reported that a bar was closing when it wasn't. Steve Rempas operated several bars, all with names that echoed one another: Loading Zone, Ozone and Loading Dock, among others. The Loading Dock was the most popular and I reported that it was closing, when in fact, it was one of his other bars that was being shuttered. Rempas called the office and screamed so loudly at his ad rep, that everyone in the office could hear. After Sherman Heinrich, the advertising manager calmed him down, I got on the phone and apologized profusely. I told Rempas I would correct it in the next issue of the magazine. The following week I led off my column with a retraction, making a joke about how similar the names were and that perhaps I'd been over-served and confused the bar names. We thought that would satisfy him. It didn't. He brought a lawsuit against the magazine and me. To settle the case Ralph promised him free advertising for any business he owned for as long as *Gay Chicago* was published. Rempas also had a large outstanding bill for advertising, which of course was eliminated. I had cost *Gay Chicago* and Ralph a lot of money.

When I was called into the conference room, I was sure I was being fired and began planning how I could back-peddle my refusals to Jeff McCourt. I was stunned when Ralph offered me a promotion. If Ralph was aware that Jeff was trying to poach me, perhaps he was anxious not to lose his most widely read columnist. Maybe he thought the strengths I brought to the magazine outweighed that one mistake. Rather than firing me, Ralph offered me a promotion. He explained that the new format was so popular they were making it a permanent change. As part of that change he wanted me to head up a new entertainment section. He offered me a substantial raise – $250 a week, up from the $50 each I was getting for my gossip and food columns. I would also be given the title of Entertainment Editor.

On top of that, I would have editorial control and a budget to hire writers to flesh out the section. I was shocked and delighted. In addition to teaching school and writing for *Gay Chicago*, for the past two years I'd been editing a trade magazine for manicurists and make-up artists. The subject bored me out of my mind, but I needed the additional income since Adam was living with me.

I accepted their offer. I worked that summer on developing the new section, which we would call "After Dark." It debuted in the Labor Day issue of 1988. I hired people who I knew were good writers and had knowledge of the arts. In addition to my friend Danny Kopelson, I also brought on John Schmid, Dave Murray, and Joe Russell. Between us, we'd cover entertainment and lifestyle features including cabaret, literature, fashion, entertaining, décor, film and theater. In retrospect, I realize the staff was exclusively white men. Given the opportunity today, I would aim for a more diverse group of writers. Over the years other writers joined us: Brian Treglown, Lynn "Kecky" Carroll and Gale Harris. Larry Brewer, a local DJ, wrote a music column, primarily about dance music in the clubs. I encouraged him to widen his scope. For the most part, the rest of the magazine consisted of calendar listings, items taken from news services and press releases and the lucrative classified section.

The first "After Dark" featured a lead story I wrote on the Miss Continental contest, the pinnacle of female impersonator competitions. Back then, we used the term drag queen, but the contestants represented a wide spectrum of the transgender population. Although the majority identified as gay, there were some straight men who dressed in drag for pleasure and/or as a profession. Some contestants were transitioning, others identified as the opposite gender but had no desire to transition. The only rule was "no bottom surgery," because once they did that, they were considered female, not female impersonators.

As an indication of my new status in the community, Jim Flint, the show's producer, asked me to be a judge at that year's Miss Continental pageant. Among my fellow judges were nationally known recording artist Phyllis Hyman and professional athletes. After judging the grueling round of interviews, evening gown, swimsuit and talent sections, I gained a greater respect for what those "girls" went through. At that point, other than a few costume parties where I threw on a wig and a dress, I'd never done drag.

My life had a new routine. After teaching each day, I'd head to the *Gay Chicago* offices and work for a few hours. Adam was in high school and after school he was supposed to go home, do his chores and homework before I arrived to make dinner at six. After dinner, Adam could go out if his chores were done. The rule was that on school nights he had to be in his bedroom by 10:00 p.m. I didn't care if he went to sleep. He was free to read, but he couldn't be out or watching TV. Some of those nights, I was out at community events or reviewing a play, but I'd always call at ten to make certain that Adam was, at the very least, home. The rule was no visitors unless I was home, but I knew he wasn't following that rule. The fact that the refrigerator was empty every third day led me to believe he was hanging around the house with his friends. Fine, I'd rather he did that than be out wandering the streets.

Most nights I got home around midnight, and if Adam was partying, he was good at cleaning it up. When we both were home, he spent most of his time in his room, either alone and on the phone, or with his best friend, Tim. Adam and I made a deal. His room was his own private space. As long as I didn't smell anything, I wouldn't go in there. One weekend when he was visiting his mother, I did notice an odor. I went in to clean and discovered what you would expect a teenage boy's room to look, a disaster zone. I decided to clean it and ran a broom under his bed. I unearthed fast-food wrappers, a pizza box, and a few used condoms. It's difficult for a parent to accept that their child has become a sexual being, but we had had the talk about safe sex, so I was glad he used condoms.

# CHAPTER 21

W hile all those changes were happening at *Gay Chicago*, I was also going through other changes. I'd been teaching in Cabrini-Green for eight years. One of the parents had seen me at the Gay Pride Parade and decided to make a stink about it. Fortunately, the Chicago Public Schools' non-discrimination policy made it difficult for her to affect my job, but it was an uncomfortable situation. I applied for a position in another school in the Humboldt Park neighborhood. When I interviewed, the principal, Burton Hirsch, turned out to be a friend of my uncle, also a Chicago Public School principal. I think that helped me get the job. Burt assigned me to a first-grade class with the top students – they still grouped by ability back then. There was a lot of gang activity in the neighborhood. The families were mostly working-class Mexicans and Puerto Ricans, who just wanted a safe school for their children. I loved that class. It was such a change to have parents who were involved in their children's education and willing to work with me. My students did well in the end of the year standardized testing. Most scored at least one year above grade level, an exceptional achievement for an inner-city classroom. The parents went to the principal and asked if I could take the class to second grade, which I was glad to do. The following year the same thing occurred. By then, most of the students going into third grade the next year were reading at the fifth or sixth-grade level. The parents asked me to take them to third, which I did. I refused to take the class any farther, as I was growing too close to them.

I grew so much as a teacher at that school. I was even named one of the state's "Most Talented Teachers" in 1993 by a performing arts organization. It amazes me now that I was doing two full-time jobs, teaching and working at *Gay Chicago*. I was also on the national board of the Gay and Lesbian Parents Group International (GLPCI) and served as its Vice President of Conference Planning. This meant, not only attending four board meetings a year, but aiding local groups in planning the annual convention.

After Dark was proving to be a popular section of the magazine. We were even getting advertising from entertainment-based companies representing theaters, films, and music. Quotes from our reviews started appearing in ads for shows. A rave from us could guarantee a good run for a play. We were respected entertainment journalists. The little bar guide was a player now. Ralph and Dan were the kind of business owners who gave back to the community. They sponsored one of the first fundraisers for an AIDS organization. I proposed a bachelor auction as a fundraiser for Chicago House, an AIDS hospice, and Ralph supported it.

---

### Cruising for a Dreamboat:

"Bachelor" auctions were nothing new – mainstream organizations had been doing them for years – but they hadn't been tried in the gay community. When planning the fundraiser, we asked community leaders to suggest single friends who'd be willing to be auctioned off as part of a date package. We solicited donations from restaurants and entertainment venues. We had each "date" photographed by Jennifer Girard, a leading commercial photographer in Chicago, who donated her time and talent. One of the riverboats that offered sightseeing cruises donated their services for the benefit. Some of the bachelors were well known in the community, but most were not. A few weeks before the event the auction was the lead story in After Dark, with information about the cruise and the date packages. We ran the photos and profiles of the 20 "eligible bachelors" participating. The benefit was a success beyond anyone's hopes. It sold out in less than a week and raised nearly $45,000, the most money raised for a local AIDS agency at the time. We repeated the event annually. There were now two major annual fundraising events I'd started.

---

The success of the After Dark section led me to start a second gossip column in which I focused on the entertainment industry in Chicago. I wrote the column under the name Bessie Mae Kulo. We even set up a separate voicemail for Bessie to get her tips. Bessie got both fan mail and hate mail.

One day there was a letter addressed to Bessie with a newspaper clipping inside. The clipping was from an article in a newspaper serving the Northwest suburbs. It was about a semi-professional theater company, Music on Stage, performing the world premiere of a new musical, written by the company's artistic director, Frank DePaul. The same Frank DePaul with whom I'd written *Spin Cycle*. He'd disappeared from the city's theater scene, so the clipping was a shock. Even more of a shock was that the play being produced was *Musical,* the last show we wrote together. It had never had a full production, just a short workshop at a small theater. After I got over the shock, I called the theater company in northwest suburban Palatine and spoke to the company's business manager. I introduced myself as the entertainment editor and asked about the play. The business manager was thrilled to speak to me, assuming I was planning on reviewing the show. At one point he said, "Yes, our artistic director is very talented, he wrote the show himself, and he's going to direct it." I asked for the director's name. "Frank DePaul," he said.

That's when I dropped the bomb. I told the business manager that I wrote the show and hadn't given my permission for its use, nor had I been paid any royalties. I said that I understood it was a small company and any royalties would be minimal. I told the business manager for Music on Stage that I had no intention of shutting down the show – it was opening in two weeks. But they'd have to send out a new press release crediting me as the author, give me 20 tickets to opening night and provide me with a videotape of the show. I also wanted to attend a rehearsal to make certain the show hadn't been altered.

You'd have thought that when I turned up for rehearsal, Frank would be embarrassed, but he wasn't. I looked over the script and found one major change. The show was originally set in the 1950s and each number was a parody of a typical Broadway song of the era. The hack director in the script keeps inserting numbers that proved successful in other musicals. So, there's a Polynesian number because *South Pacific* was a hit, and a bobby-soxer number to imitate *Bye Bye Birdie*. Frank moved the show to the present, so none of those references made sense. However, there was nothing the small company could do to correct the change at that late date, so I let them continue.

I brought my group of 20 friends to the opening night performance and got a copy of the video, as agreed. That was the clincher. I left working in theater for good. I'd enjoy it from the other side of the footlights, and never have to deal with the infighting, egos, and dishonesty again.

I never saw Frank again until my old roommate Kelvin's wedding. By then Frank had lost his lover Scott to AIDS and was barely holding on himself at that point. I wish I could say that I was able to forgive him, but I never did.

# CHAPTER 22

## ✳ ✳ ✳

A
t home, I was having more and more problems with Adam. Although bright and artistic, he was never a motivated student. When he graduated from 8ᵗʰ grade and was ready to move on to high school, it was clear he wasn't going to get into any of the better schools. I didn't want him going to our neighborhood school because of gang activity. He ended up choosing Roosevelt High School because they offered a specialty in computer science, a new area at the time. I think Adam assumed he'd be playing video games all day. I had gone to Roosevelt and one of my favorite teachers, Linda Kaplan, was still on staff. I called her and asked her if she would put in a good word for Adam.

Even though Linda was teaching girls' P.E. when I was in high school, we worked together on the committee to create an after-school social center, and we became close. It's no exaggeration to say that she is the reason I made it through high school alive. I was a popular kid and managed to get along with all the various sub-groups in our high school: the "greasers"; what we called "doopers" (preppy types); brainy kids; those in special ed (I was proficient at language arts, but math was beyond me); and jocks – when I entered high school I was 5' 10" and 175 lb., a goliath in my high school, which had a high percentage of Asian and Jewish students. I was immediately assigned to the football team where I lasted one practice. I was known for being funny and, if anyone thought I was gay, I was never teased about it. I may have been a bit fey, but my large size and deep baritone voice didn't fit the gay stereotype.

Despite being popular and moving with the "in" crowd, there were many times I considered suicide. Part of it was the emotional abuse from my father – the physical abuse stopped when I started punching back. I'm sure much of it had to do with my conflicts about my sexuality. But the major factor was my undiagnosed bipolar disorder. I spent many mornings and afternoons in Linda's office crying uncontrollably. She always managed to calm me down. As our friendship developed over the years, I discovered she had an affinity for gay men. I hate the term "fag hag." But as it's used, it applied to Linda; she loved gay men and was a big sister to a number of them. I sensed that. That's why I confided in her. Although we never discussed my attraction to boys, I told her about every other problem I had.

Linda was now a school counselor and promised me she'd keep an eye on Adam. So, every morning on my way to work, I dropped Adam off and watched him walk into my alma mater. I'd drive to school and about mid-morning, I'd receive a page from the office that there was a message waiting for me. I'd stop in during my break and find a note from Linda, telling me that Adam had cut a class – or more likely, classes. Then Adam and I repeated the same dance; he'd claim he was being bullied. I'd call the school and discover Adam was lying. Around that time, I was having our house painted and one day the painter said, "I don't know if it's my business, but I think you should know. Your son comes home about 11 every morning and he and his friends hang out all day. They leave around five and Adam spends the time cleaning up before you get home from work."

No wonder the refrigerator was always empty. I attributed that to the fact that his best friend Tim Westbrooks, whose mother couldn't care for him, was practically living with us and that teenage boys were big eaters. Or that they had friends over the nights I was out. I felt betrayed. After years of our being a team, it was devastating to find out he was lying to me. I knew Adam had some issues; I'd been taking him to a therapist for a few years. Sometimes he would shut down, and I couldn't get through to him. I put it down to teenage hormones and resentment about the divorce. I thought it was a difficult period, but that we'd get through it. In retrospect, I resented Adam, blaming him for the relationship between Chuck and I not working out. Although, I now know, after years of therapy, it was only the instigating factor. As we argued, things escalated. A lot of Adam's frustrations came to the surface, and in the heat of the moment, I reached out and slapped him.

I had never spanked Adam when he was a child. The look of resentment and fury on his face scared me. I'd always promised myself I wouldn't be like my father. Adam struck back, and I grabbed him and held him tight, apologizing over and over. I sent him to his room so that we could both cool off. I went upstairs to my bedroom and after sobbing into a towel for 15 minutes, I called his mother. During the years Adam lived with me, she, her husband and two kids, had moved to a far-flung suburb. She was a stay-at-home mother. I explained the situation and told her that Adam needed more supervision than I could provide. For once we agreed on something and Adam moved back with her.

Was it the right decision? I still don't know. The path Adam was taking was a dangerous one. When I told him what his mother and I decided, I saw his eyes go dead. I almost backed down. But I knew that a suburban school was better for him. There were temptations there too, but at least he wouldn't be able to skip school and hop on public transportation, as he did in the city. Since he didn't drive, he had to rely on the school bus, and his mother would keep a close eye on him.

After he moved, I phoned two to three times a week, but he wouldn't take my calls. He refused to see me. After a few months, his mother reported to me that he had a B average, much better than when he was living with me. We didn't speak to each other again until his graduation day. I asked him if I could take him and a few friends out to lunch after the ceremony. I drove out with his best friend, Tim. The boys had remained close, talking on the phone all the time. Both decided to enter the service, having been seduced by the movie *Top Gun*. I warned them that military service wouldn't be anything like in the film, that they wouldn't be spending their days playing volleyball on the beach. They refused to listen but found out later for themselves. I think it was the right decision because it forced them both to learn two important things: self-discipline and how to take orders.

Adam and I eventually rebuilt our relationship. We had a long discussion about my decision to send him to live with his mother; he told me he thought it was because he was in my way. When I explained my reasoning, that was the beginning of repairing the break between us. After his service, he lived with me for a few weeks, until he found his own apartment. Tim ended up living with me while he went to college. It was like I had two sons. Adam and I are very close to this day.

# CHAPTER 23

It seemed as if everything was going well, and it was, professionally. However, I was struggling with depression again. I'd put on weight when Chuck and I were together, as many people do when they settle into a relationship. With Adam gone, the house was so quiet, I went out almost every night. I could justify it; after all, I was an entertainment editor and gossip columnist. I had to be out there to report on things. It was also fun being treated as a celebrity, albeit a minor one. If I walked into a bar or club, a manager came over to find me the best seat in the house and ply me with drinks. I'd walk in and hear people saying my name and casting glances at me. As a result, I was drinking more than I ever had. Thankfully drugs never had any appeal to me, but I developed a taste for vodka. I'd go out to the clubs and bars every night for events and, since most bartenders liked seeing their name in my gossip column, they offered me free drinks. Then on the way home, I'd stop and get some sort of greasy "drunk food." Between teaching, writing for the magazine and serving on the board of GPCI, I was continuously dashing from one meeting to the next. In between I'd grab fast food meals. I've always struggled with my weight, so now I was nearly 250 lbs. I was masking the loneliness with food.

I was also facing the fact that I was getting older. This was demonstrated to me at a dinner party hosted by Dave Edwards, owner of

Gentry, the most popular piano bar in town. It was a sign of my increased status that I was invited. The other guys – no women, all guys – were much better off than I was. I don't know if they were the A list crowd, but they were indeed a few levels above the crowd I usually socialized with. The seating arrangement was older rich gay men and pretty younger man pairings. The eye candy seated next to me was a cocktail waiter at Dave's bar. We chatted as dinner went on. In the course of our conversation, I mentioned that I was a teacher. He replied that he remembered having a crush on a male pre-school teacher. It didn't take long to connect the dots. I'd worked at the university's pre-school when I was an undergrad and had been his teacher. I never felt so old! Here I'd been flirting with this young man. I went home very depressed.

The tipping point came when I went on vacation with my friend Alyn Toler. Alyn was gorgeous and would later go on to win the Mr. Windy City contest. But he was also a sweet man. Our relationship wasn't romantic – although I wouldn't have minded that – we were just close friends. I was offered the chance to stay at a resort near South Beach, Florida. It had been one of those hotels where old Jewish ladies spent the winter. However, the hotel's new owners wanted to capitalize on the growing cachet of South Beach. They thought if they advertised in gay papers, they'd get the gay business. They invited me to spend a week as their guest. I invited Alyn to join me, and we arrived the day after Christmas for a week-long stay.

The minute we arrived at the hotel, I realized it was a lost cause. They hadn't renovated, and the hotel pool was filled with old ladies doing water aerobics. No self-respecting queen would ever stay there. Alyn took one look at the "gym" with its exercise belts and other old lady equipment and walked out. He found a real gym on nearby Lincoln Road and signed up for a one-week membership. That night we went out clubbing. I was used to people in Chicago fawning on me. In Miami, I was just a fat queen standing next to a pretty boy. At the end of that first night, I was in tears. Alyn wasn't having any of my self-pity. He'd been a chubby growing up and said the only way I was going to change was by working out and eating better. He made me join the gym and work out with him. Of course, trying to keep up with him, I overdid it and tore a bicep. For six months, I couldn't even open a door with my right arm.

When we returned to Chicago, Alyn helped me improve my diet and choose a workout regime that suited me. Weight training was out as I found it tedious, and I had that torn bicep, but I loved aerobics classes. Now my routine was teaching, followed by working at *Gay Chicago* for two hours a day, then off to the gym for an hour of aerobics, then home for a healthy dinner. Sometimes I even went running after dinner. When I went out, I sipped white wine or just club soda. By June, I was down to 180 lbs, had a 30" waist – which I packed into 29" jeans – and actually showed a little definition, though I was by no means muscular. I felt better than I had in years.

I also decided to shape up *Gay Chicago*. After the blow-up between Ralph and Danny Sotomayor, we lost another writer, Paul Adams, a former Mr. Windy City and an AIDS activist. He quit in solidarity with Danny. *Outlines* and *Windy City Times* both ran big stories about what happened. Rex Wockner, a columnist at *Outlines,* wrote, "*Gay Chicago* employees warned Sotomayor that his cartoons would be pulled as soon as Di Leo died because Gernhardt and other magazine management vehemently opposed Sotomayor's politics."

I don't know who those employees were. However, Ralph and Jerry Williams, our business manager, were big supporters of Mayor Daley, often a target of Danny's anger and rage. So I suppose the statement was true. That may have been where Danny got the idea that I had something to do with his dismissal. I guess he saw me as the "other magazine management." I was about as apolitical as you could be, other than standing up for social justice, I tended to stay out of the political arena.

As far as I was concerned, the loss of Danny's voice was a big blow to *Gay Chicago*, but I felt he was a better fit at *Windy City Times*. We were still an entertainment guide and had little to do with politics. We also skewed to an older, more conservative readership. To inject some fresh opinions, and to help me avoid slipping back into bad habits, I gave up my gossip column. I turned it over to one of our ad sales guys, Dave Myler. I also brought on younger writers to work on After Dark.

Tracy Baim was also trying to turn the tide at her publication. She was still battling the perception that *Outlines* was a "lesbian" newspaper. True her paper did cover women's issues more often than either *Gay Chicago* or *Windy City Times*, but not enough to justify being labeled as solely a "women's paper." Whether true or not, Jeff had painted that image of her and she couldn't shake it off. Instead, Baim started a second publication, a digest-sized entertainment weekly. *Nightlines*, as she titled it, debuted at the end of March 1990. It featured most of the same columnists and writers as *Outlines* and picked up Paul Adams from us. It also featured a gossip column written by Mary McCauley, a former nun who wrote the column under the name Mother Superior. She never quite got the tone correct. Instead of sounding like she was giving juicy gossip, her column always read like a school newsletter.

*Nightlines* ran the typical bar listings of drink specials, social group meetings, and a few pictures taken at clubs and bars. It also had a news digest and a column by Rex Wockner, where he wrote about having sex in public places. All in all, it was a dull publication. The fact that Baim packed as many words on a page as she could, didn't make it too exciting to look at either.

Baim took niche marketing a step further and published *Black Lines,* a magazine geared toward African American gays and lesbians. With all of Baim's publications having the word "line" in the title – *Outlines, Night Lines, Black Lines* – we joked that she was starting a magazine for lesbian cat owners called *Felines.* Instead, she published *En La Vida* for the gay Hispanic community. Again, the content was of high quality. They were both respectable publications, offering voices to disenfranchised communities. The problem was the design; both were packed with information, but little of visual interest.

# CHAPTER 24

Although Chicago's first case of AIDS was identified as early as 1981, for the most part the rates of diagnosed infections was lower than on the east and west coasts. My friend and therapist, John Rouse, was the first person I lost to AIDS. From the time I heard he was sick until the time he died, was just a few short days. At that time, I'd barely heard of the disease. John was admitted to the hospital where I worked as a pediatric therapist. I visited him the day after his admission, and when I stopped by the next day, he was gone. At the time we didn't know it was AIDS; the term wasn't in use yet. We thought it was just a horrific freak illness, a rare form of cancer.

However, by the mid-1980s, AIDS was always in the news, and people you casually knew, were there one day and dead the next. Suddenly, the phrase we used to describe a huge penis, "the dick of death" was no longer appropriate. Nor was making jokes about STDs. The time between diagnosis and death was short, sometimes as little as a week. If you saw someone who'd lost a lot of weight, you no longer congratulated them, you worried about them.

Young people tend to think they're invulnerable. The gay community quickly became aware of its mortality. Still, I was lucky, I didn't lose anyone else close to me until the fall of 1988. I first read obituaries for friends of mine in the September 9 edition of *Windy City Times*: Bob Krause and Steve Brahill.

Steve and his lover Pat Kasaras opened Chicago's first modern gay bar, Christopher Street. Unlike bars in the past, Christopher Street featured large windows, an indication that the community was no longer afraid to be seen. Steve and Pat were charming and handsome; both had big smiles and massive muscles, but their hearts were even bigger. Whenever I approached them about a fundraiser, they always offered to host it, make a donation, or volunteer. Steve got sick first and, in what seemed the blink of an eye, was gone. Pat was around a few years longer, but eventually he succumbed to the disease as well.

In 1989 men I cared for began to fall like dominoes; Dan Di Leo, my friend Gabor, a talented artist, my good friend Paul Wenson, who I met through the gay parents' group and who I lived with while working on my house. So many acquaintances from the Gay Men's Chorus and sports teams were all diagnosed and died soon after. Then, in 1990 I was hit with more losses; my good friend John Becker, and Vito Russo, the author of *The Celluloid Closet* with whom I'd had a fling. Suddenly there were more and more people with whom I had sex with dying from AIDS-related diseases. I got myself checked every few months. Somehow, I was always negative.

Although I was not the type to take part in ACT UP protests, I knew they were necessary. The government was doing nothing. Our community needed to take care of its own. I did what I did best and covered every AIDS benefit and event. I also organized and volunteered for benefits. I participated in the display of the Names Project quilt at Navy Pier and had the honor of introducing Jessye Norman as the opening reader of names. My birthday gatherings at Sidetrack continued and the 1991 event raised $2,500 for Stop AIDS. It featured performances by the She-Devils, a troupe of square-dancing drag queens and an appearance by "Cruisin' for a Dreamdate" bachelors, to promote the event.

---

### Titles and Awards

The Mr. Windy City Contest was a beauty pageant of sorts. Gay bars and businesses held contests or appointed a contestant for the final event, held at the Park West night theater. The evening was an excuse to ogle handsome men in skimpy bathing suits – although they also modeled casual wear and formal attire. The winner took home a sash, a trophy, and a cash award. It was basically a promotion for the bars by *Gay Chicago* (*Windy City Times* wasn't around when it started, or they might have chosen a different name). The title meant nothing other than to those who won it, it was basically no more than a beauty contest. That was until 1988. That year, Paul Adams, a Navy vet, turned the position into a jumping-off point for activism. He used his new-found notoriety to promote community organization and AIDS fundraising. The contest continued for a few more years with the winners now committing to raise funds for community agencies.

To fill up time during the contest, *Gay Chicago* also honored community leaders and businesses by presenting "The Gay Chicago Awards." It was mostly PR for the magazine and presented advertisers with awards such as "Best Disco," "Best DJ," "Best Bartender," "Best Drag Queen," etc. But it wasn't all fluff, they also gave out awards honoring community leaders such as "Organizer of the Year" and "Man of the Year" and "Woman of the Year."

In 1990 I convinced Ralph that we should also present After Dark awards to honor outstanding achievement in Chicago theater and cabaret. The After Dark staff writers nominated and selected the winners for the best performances and productions in town.

The After Dark Awards were unusual in that we didn't differentiate between large and small companies. A storefront production would compete with a touring Broadway show. Theater people love to get awards, so they all showed up to claim the plaque, with a beautiful logo designed by Lori Dana, a volunteer at AIDS Foundation Chicago. It was a huge success.

The only negative comments, cited by letters to the editor in both *Gay Chicago* and *Windy City Times*, called Ralph Paul and local businessman Jim Flint on the carpet for their unprofessional behavior while hosting the Mr. Windy City Contest. Both appeared to be inebriated – they denied it – and fondled contestants and made inappropriate remarks.

The After Dark Awards were proudly displayed in the lobbies of winning theaters and cited by actors in their program bios. The following year, to avoid the problems with Ralph and Jim, I suggested the After Dark Awards became a stand-alone event. I also suggested it be a fundraiser for the AIDS Foundation. That first year of our stand-alone ceremony, we honored Karen Mason and Brian Lasser with the Legacy Award. Karen and Brian started their careers at Le Pub, a gay cabaret, before moving on to New York. Brian died of

AIDS related causes soon after we presented him with the award. Karen went on to become one of New York's top cabaret acts, winning the MAC Award numerous years in a row. She starred in hit Broadway shows such as *Mama Mia*, *Hairspray*, and *Sunset Boulevard*. The After Dark Awards continued throughout my years at *Gay Chicago*, always as a benefit for an AIDS organization.

# CHAPTER 25

The magazine was thriving, and the After Dark staff continued to grow. Two of the "Cruisin' for a Dreamdate" bachelors, Alyn Toler and Dr. Steve Lasik, started writing columns for the magazine. Alyn's was on hair and working out, he was a model and hairstylist. Steve, an osteopath, wrote a medical advice column. Toler was a former Mr. Windy City who donated many hours to charities and fundraisers. He also co-founded the Pink Angels, a group that patrolled the streets to reduce "gay-bashings," which had increased as the AIDS crisis stirred up fear and hatred. In a strange irony, Alyn later became angry with me, and the rest of the folks at *Gay Chicago*, for no reason that I could discern. I think that as he battled AIDS, his thought processes were affected. Over the years, I saw this with other friends in the latter stages of the disease. They often made irrational decisions. One of my friends from the parents group left town and a strong support system to take a menial job without benefits in Boston, where he knew very few people. Danny Kopelson's husband, John Coleman, once drove erratically with a car full of passengers. Although they did not have full-blown dementia, their impulse control and decision-making skills were impaired. When that happened, there was little we, as friends, without medical power of attorney, could do.

Steve Lasik's stint with us was too short. Soon after he started writing his column, he found out he had AIDS. Knowing the probable outcome, he chose to end his life by hanging himself. Our community lost many people in the first few years of the AIDS crisis. *Gay Chicago*'s long-time ad sales manager, Sherman Heinrich, also passed away.

But there were fun times as well. I swore I would do drag and perform a number on stage before I turned 40. Paula Sinclaire and Vikki Spykke, two drag queens who performed at many of my birthday parties, invited me to join their show at a bar called The North End. I accepted and one of the bar's customers, a make-up artist and hairstylist offered to help "do" me. On March 21, just a week after my 39th birthday, Charity Case made her debut. I chose the name since I was donating my tips to charity (The Dan Di Leo PWA Fund). However, I forgot that I was also committed to attend a concert by the Windy City Gay Chorus at the Chicago Theater that night. The drag show wasn't until 10:30, so I had to attend the concert in full drag, then dash out to perform at the bar immediately afterward. Leave it to me to make my drag debut at the Chicago Theater.

I attended the concert in a skin-tight shimmery black dress, black opera gloves, a gold lame wrap, and an auburn wig! I was in a skinny phase then, thank God! Of course, being March in Chicago, it snowed that day and there was a sheet of ice covering the sidewalk. It was a miracle I made it from the car to the theater in six-inch heels without killing myself. Later that evening I did two numbers in the show, one of which was Patti Austin's version of *I Can Cook, Too* from *On the Town*. It seemed every "celebrity" in the community showed up for my debut and my tips for the night brought in hundreds of dollars for the charity.

During all this, the game of musical chairs at the various gay publications continued. Tracy Baim may not have been as mercurial as Jeff McCourt, but she was demanding and was known to lose her temper. Staff leapt from one publication to another. Mary McCauley, aka Mother Superior, left *Outlines* to join *Windy City Times*. Jon-Henri Damski, an odd duck who wrote pieces that could only be described as vignettes of gay life, worked for each of the papers at one point or another. Lynn Kecky Carroll had written entertainment pieces for Jeff and was one of the people I hired when we started After Dark. She wasn't getting enough work from us and returned to *Windy City Times*. Jeff also hired a local writer, Kelly Harmon, as his Entertainment Editor. She lasted a few weeks and then disappeared from the scene.

While McCourt and Baim continued their feud, we at *Gay Chicago* held onto our role as the neutral party. McCourt was starting to self-implode, so I stayed out of his way, except for a charity event at Roscoe's bar. Somebody came up with the idea to host an event based upon the television show *Family Feud* and invited two of the publications to send teams to compete. *Windy City Times* was represented by Mother Superior (Mary McCauly) and staff writers Dan Perreten, Melanie Holps, Steen Lawson and David Olsen. I was joined by After Dark contributors Jeff Glass, Larry Brewer, Gale Harris, a friend from my days in the Gay Parents' Group, and John David, our first writer of color. We raised funds for the Gerber-Hart Library.

---

## People I lost to AIDS

Chicago was luckier than some big cities. By the time AIDS became a full-blown epidemic in the Midwest, there were medications that prolonged, then saved, lives. I hesitate to list those I lost to AIDS because I'm sure to forget someone. However, my experience living through this plague compels me to remember those that didn't survive. Some of these people were close friends. Some I've written about in this book. Some were not much more than acquaintances, but all touched my life in some way.

| | | |
|---|---|---|
| Paul Adams. | Robert Adams | Billy Albiez |
| Ortez Alderson | Joe Alongi | Paul A. Anderson |
| Ron Anderson | Albert 'Alana Russell' Arteese | Ted Bales |
| Michael Barto | Bob Bearden | John Becker |
| David Bell | Jeff Bivona | Ray Blevins |
| Allan (Baby Cheeks) Boyd | Bob Brady | Stephen Brahill |
| Wayne Buidens | Thom Callahan | Richard Cash |
| R.J. Chaffin | Chris Clason | Jerrold Cohen |
| Bobby Cook | John Coleman | Chris Cothran |
| Jerry Crawford | Rich Davis | Sam Davis |
| Frank DePaul | Dan Di Leo | Thom Dombkowski |

| | | |
|---|---|---|
| Eddie Dugan | David Navarro Edmonds | Faron Evans |
| Robb Evans | Robert Ford | Bon Foster |
| Gabor | Ron Geiman | Marty Gigele |
| Aaron Gold | Frank Goley | Ida Greathouse |
| Joe Gregg | George 'Dick' Guenther | Garth Guido |
| James 'Jimmy' Guth | John Hammell | Sherman Heinrich |
| Chris Hickey | Sam Hill | Joseph Holmes |
| Diana Hutton | Bob Janatta | Rich Jeffries |
| Ray Johnson | Patrick Kasaras | Michael K |
| DeJon Karlae | Joe Kontoff | Brant Larson |
| Steve Lasik | Brian Lasser | Chip Mathews |
| Kelly Michaels | Chicago Molly | Scott Mullen |
| Tom Neniskes | Carl Occhipinti | Dom Orejudos |
| Passionella | Laird Peterson | Larry Dante Prospero |
| Jon Reich | Lon Rice | John Rouse |
| Vito Russo | Ron Sable | Dale Sapper |
| Bill Sawicki | John Schmid | Dean Schroeder |
| Bobby Shelton | Larry Sloan | Danny Sotomayor |
| Gregory Sprague | Paul Stensland | Tim Sullivan |
| Scotty Thompson | Butch Toland | Allyn Toler |
| Tom Triplett | Ussi | Mark Vanesco |
| Rene Van Hulle | Paul Varnell | Al Wardell |
| Paul Wenson | Dale Wouk | Ronald Ziebarth |

... and I'm sure there are more that I never knew I lost.

# CHAPTER 26

At this point, my life consisted of teaching, working at *Gay Chicago,* and exercising. Part of that routine was running along the lakefront. For the first time in my life, I was happy being single. I would see many of the same people during the run and we'd nod a note of recognition and continue on our ways. One evening, I spied one of the men I regularly saw riding his bike. He was sitting on a bench along the path examining the chain of his bike. I'd always thought he was attractive, though he seemed a little too much of the protest-activist type for me. It was late fall and he was wearing a leather jacket. It was unzipped, and underneath I saw a t-shirt for a punk band. I thought we probably had nothing in common, but he was too cute to pass by. Stalling for an opportunity to meet him, I stopped at the other end of the bench and leaned over the retie my shoe. Also letting him see how nice my butt looked in my Lycra running shorts. I turned back, ready to start my run and saw he had taken off his jacket and was fiddling with the bike.

"Anything wrong?" I asked, as if I would know what to do if there were. He was wearing a long-sleeve T-shirt underneath the punk band shirt. He was slim and had beautiful blue eyes. We flirted and made a date to meet at Big Chicks, a local gay bar, later that evening and then go out for dinner. I turned around, ran toward home, showered and shaved. I didn't have to do much to make the house presentable. Now that I lived alone, Helen, my Polish cleaning lady, usually found the house almost exactly as she had left it after her last visit. She'd just been there that day, so everything was spotless. I put on my date night underwear, a pair of tight jeans and ran out the door to my date.

I walked into Big Chick's a few minutes before I was supposed to meet this guy. Was his name Craig or Gregg? I couldn't remember. I've never been good with names. Working for *Gay Chicago*, I met a lot of people. I could never remember all their names, so I started calling everyone darling or honey. I arrived at Big Chicks early, so if there was anyone there that I knew, I could get the chatter out of the way. I didn't want to take a chance that this guy was a "star-fucker." Not that I was much of a star; few people recognized my face, but almost everyone in Chicago's LGBTQ community knew my name. Of course, he was sitting there, already holding a cocktail – rum and Coke I guessed. For once, I didn't know anyone in the bar, except the bartender, who knew I was a friend of Michelle Fire, the owner. I bought my drink, and we moved to a secluded area to talk.

I introduced myself as Rick (no last name), and it turned out he was Gregg, not Craig. As we chatted, I discovered we had more in common than I thought: a love of books, movies, and music. Although his taste tended toward more esoteric fare and mine was standard gay-boy stuff; dance music and show tunes. We both were writers, although I knew nothing about his genre, poetry. Best of all, he recognized my name but didn't seem to care either way. He'd worked for a gay paper, *The Washington Blade*, while he was in grad school, so he wasn't impressed by the supposed glamour of the business.

At an awkward pause in the conversation, I leaned in and kissed him. This man could kiss. It was electric. Although it wasn't the *Some Enchanted Evening* moment I'd had with Chris and Chuck, there was an attraction there. When we took each other's hands, I felt this was meant to be. We had talked about going to dinner, but I suggested we go to my place instead. We were barely in the door before we were clawing the clothes off each other. We spent hours making love, but I had to get up to teach in the morning. At about 11 p.m., I reluctantly sent him home. It was the Tuesday before Thanksgiving. As I walked him to the door, we made plans for that Friday night.

For our Friday night date, I suggested Heartland Café, a local health food restaurant. I found it to be a great first date spot. It was gay-friendly, but not populated by the bar types who I met through *Gay Chicago*. It turned out to be the perfect place, as Gregg was a vegetarian. I scored a point on that one. I perused the wine list and asked if he preferred red or white. He said that he didn't drink. A warning flag went up. I didn't want to date another man with a drinking problem. I asked if he was in recovery and said that if he were, I wouldn't order anything for myself. He told me he just never developed a taste for it and ordered a Coke. Point for him! During our discussion he admitted he was only in town until the end of the year, when he'd be moving back to the East Coast. My heart sank, but I decided to enjoy the time with him while it lasted. Also, it never hurt to have an ex-boyfriend in another city.

We spent every evening together after that. I was even invited to his family's Hanukkah party. Gregg's family was warm and welcoming. It wasn't just his immediate family; all his cousins were there as well. I found out later that although the group numbered nearly 50, it was only his father's side of the family.

One of the best things I discovered was that he had women friends, as did I. Because of teaching, most of my co-workers were women, but even in high school, I had more female friends than male ones. I especially loved his best friend Allison Nichol, a force of nature, and what the women's community refers to as a soft butch. We spent New Year's Eve with Allison and her partner Gay and some other friends of Gregg. After dinner at Dellwood Pickle, an Andersonville restaurant, we went back to Allison and Gay's apartment to drink a toast at midnight. It was a bittersweet night, for I knew in a few weeks Gregg was leaving town. I'd started this as a casual fling, but as we kissed at midnight, I whispered in his ear, "Marry me. Stay here, and I'll move east with you as soon as I can."

I was as surprised by my offer as Gregg was. Was I really ready to give up everything I'd worked so hard to achieve? Although I loved teaching, the principal at my school had retired and been replaced by a man who was not as supportive of an openly gay teacher on his staff. I'd been looking for a different school, but at my pay level, it was hard to find a position.

I was growing disenchanted with my "fame" and, while I loved working at *Gay Chicago*, I was ready to step away. I barely saw my sister, and Adam had enlisted with the Marines and lived in Georgia now, so why not move? I could take early retirement. I had nearly 20 years with the board of education. Surely my pension, when combined with a teaching salary elsewhere and whatever office job Gregg got, would be able to support us.

Gregg agreed to stay. There were six months left on his lease, and if he stayed, he wouldn't have to break it and lose his security deposit. I never said either of us was romantic. Gregg and I are compatible, even though our opposite tastes from food to music make it seem otherwise. In everything that mattered, we were a perfect match. Not to mention that I found his furry body very sexy. Other than one of Gregg's ex-boyfriends, I meshed with everyone he knew, and he was the same with my crowd. I even became quite friendly with two of his exes, and we still visit them on vacations often!

# CHAPTER 27

G regg was using his old apartment as an office, spending a couple of hours a day writing there after a full day at his day job. In April of 1993, there was another March on Washington. Gregg and I planned to go. We'd heard there was going to be a mass "wedding." It would be a symbolic ceremony since same-sex marriage wasn't legal at that point. Gregg and I decided to take part to show our commitment to each other. I didn't want to make a big deal about it. I had not been in many long-term relationships, so I suggested we invite a few close friends. Then, after we'd lived together a year and felt more secure in our relationship, we could have a bigger commitment ceremony in Chicago for our families and friends.

Keeping our ceremony quiet and including only a few close friends proved to be a bigger problem than we anticipated. It turned out that *People Magazine* wanted to feature a couple taking part in the mass marriage. They called various LGBTQ papers around the country trying to find a couple to include in the profile. When they called *Gay Chicago*, Ralph, who knew about our plans, suggested they contact us. There was only one problem: while Gregg was "kind of" out to his family, the words, "I'm gay" were never said. They certainly had to know, Gregg was with one of his exes for 12 years and they moved to and from Boston together. Gregg decided we should go ahead, and his mother and family would just have to deal with it. We told the representative from *People Magazine* that we would participate.

We flew to Washington, D.C. on April 23rd, a Friday. We stayed with friends of Gregg's from his days living in D.C., Taylor and Bill. They lived in a tri-level townhouse, two doors down from Congressman Barney Frank. On Saturday morning, *People Magazine* sent a limo to pick us up. It took us to the Mayflower Hotel, where we were treated to brunch and met the writer and photographer assigned to our story. The photographer left early for the Natural History Museum, where the mass wedding was taking place, to set up and scope out a spot where he would get the best shots. As we nervously ate brunch, the reporter interviewed us and had us sign releases.

When we arrived at the museum, our friends were waiting for us. Thank goodness we arrived in a limo, it made it easy for them to find us – remember, this was before cell phones. Our friends included Allison and her best friend Kathleen Sweeney, along with two friends of Gregg's; Ellen Collins and Kim Roberts, who I was meeting for the first time. They walked with us to the area the photographer had roped off. The fact that we had an area cordoned off for us and that we arrived with an "entourage" made many of the media covering the event assume we were of some importance. As Rev. Troy Perry, founder of the Metropolitan Community Church, conducted the ceremony for 1,500 couples, sweat ran down the back of my neck. I don't know if it was nerves, the press coverage, or the combination of unseasonably warm weather and a wool sport coat, but my back was drenched by the time the singer Michael Callen performed his song *Love Don't Need A Reason.*

After the ceremony, we all went out for lunch and champagne before returning to Taylor and Bill's townhouse for a party. Attending the party was one of Gregg's ex-boyfriends, Father Michael! I felt a little intimidated at the prospect of meeting one of Gregg's exes, much less one who was a priest. However, Michael and I hit it off immediately and he and his husband Patrick are still good friends of ours. Taylor and Bill's neighbor, Barney Frank, was also having a party and the neighborhood was filled with celebrities and politicians. The next day we joined my friends from the Gay and Lesbian Parents Coalition International to take part in the march. The 1993 March on Washington resonated with me even more than the previous march in 1987. The sheer number of people was one reason. Another was the participation by so many mainstream celebrities (I walked next to Whoopi Goldberg!) What made this historical event so special, was that I was sharing it with a man I pledged to spend the rest of my life with. I was also surrounded by friends I cared about.

We returned home the next day, to find our answering machines filled with calls from friends around the country, telling us our picture was on the front page of their local paper. We ended up on the front pages of the *Denver Post*, *Los Angeles Times* and *The Washington Post*. Gregg's mother was relieved that we weren't on the cover of the Chicago papers and even more relieved when our photos were bumped from *People Magazine*. The March on Washington took place a few days before the Branch Davidian shoot-out in Waco, Texas. *People's* coverage of the March on Washington ended up being a small photograph of actress Judith Light. Gregg's mother's relief was short-lived, as the photographer sold one of the pictures to a "stock book." Art directors used stock books for photos to accompany articles. Our picture ended up accompanying articles in *Business Week* and *Elle* magazine. For years afterwards, if anyone did an Internet search using the words gay and marriage or wedding, our picture popped up.

# CHAPTER 28

Gregg and I settled into a routine. We'd converted one side of the top floor of our house into an office for him, while I had a desk in our bedroom. Gregg worked an office job during the day, but he was (and still is) an incredibly talented writer of poetry and prose. And quite disciplined. He would come home from his day job and begin writing immediately until I called him down for dinner. After dinner, he would go back to writing, while I worked on articles for *Gay Chicago* or graded my students' papers. I was happy with the routine and didn't miss going to the bars and clubs all the time. I was older – 40! – and couldn't stay out late and still teach effectively.

I announced in my next column that I was looking for a younger writer to work with. I asked those interested to submit sample columns. The After Dark section was so successful that most of my time was taken up with managerial duties, assigning and editing columns, invoicing for payroll, and doing the layout and paste-up of the section. My stepping back from the column wasn't the only change at *Gay Chicago*. When Dan died, Jerry Williams took over the business end of the magazine. Nancy Reiff, the one-time liaison to Mayor Daley, came on as Jerry's assistant. After the Sotomayer fiasco, Nancy was fired by the mayor and was unable to find a job. She called Ralph, who was always a soft touch. I think he felt responsible, so he created a job for her –

advertising director. I don't think Nancy did much more than schmooze with a few lesbian business owners and hang around the office during its infamous "cocktail hour(s)."

The folks at *Gay Chicago* liked to drink. They'd work until six, and then, as if a timer went off, they'd head to the kitchen where there was a fully stocked bar. They'd make a cocktail and head back to whatever work they were doing. The next few hours were a mixture of work and cocktail party. There were always a few hangers-on – young, pretty boys who showed up in time for the free booze. At about nine or ten, they'd lock up the office, head to a bar and continue the party. Many advertising fees were paid in trade for bar tabs. There was enough advertising revenue coming in via phone sex and pharmaceutical ads that money wasn't an issue. *Gay Chicago Magazine* was one of the few publications where I was always paid in full and on time, so all that carousing didn't seem to hurt the bottom line. It was just a bit too much for me.

# CHAPTER 29

I had long suspected that one of my writers, John Schmid, was also writing for Tracy Baim's *Outlines*. I even called Tracy and asked point-blank if he was. She denied it. I also asked John and told him if he had, it was all right as long as he didn't do it again. I was willing to give him a break. John was my friend when I hired him. He worked as a teacher at a prestigious private school and was a wonderful writer. When the school discovered he had AIDS, they fired him on the spot. Today he would have some legal recourse, but back then, he didn't. Luckily a friend of his got him a job at a local theater company. Normally, I would have made him stop writing about theater, because of the conflict of interest, but he needed both salaries, so I assigned him only the national touring shows and let it go.

However, I began to detect changes in his behavior. He started making terrible decisions; he quit his job at the theater company, where they let him work only when he felt up to it. They kept him on staff and provided health insurance. Instead, he took a job that was physically taxing and provided no health benefits. He got upset and flew off the handle at our staff meetings. He was acting recklessly.

One night I was attending a play at a local company, reviewing it because one of my writers got sick. I saw John pick up tickets from the box

# PAPER CUTS

office. That wasn't unusual. Theater companies often invited our entire staff, hoping to increase their chances of being nominated for an After Dark Award. John seemed rattled to see me, which aroused my suspicions. I went to the box office and told the clerk I thought I knew the man who just picked up a ticket but forgot his name. She told me the pseudonym he used when he wrote his reviews for *Outlines*. I called him the next day, offered him a chance to stop and begged him to see a therapist. He refused and hung up on me. I reluctantly called him back and told him he was fired. John died a short time later. I don't know whether his self-destructive behavior hastened his demise or not.

To replace John, I hired someone I knew from the theater and cabaret circuit, Jeff Rossen. Jeff was a reliable writer and a great reviewer of theater, although he often let his personal relationships with the actors or cabaret performers cloud his judgment. But I was also guilty of that.

I was happy at home and things were going well at *Gay Chicago*. However, my teaching career was becoming less and less enjoyable. I enjoyed my colleagues and it was empowering having a principal who stood behind an openly gay teacher. Most of the parents were supportive, but there were always a few trying to make it into an issue. Burt squashed any problems before they even had a chance to blossom. After I was hired, he brought on three more openly gay teachers, including my friend Rob Evans. After Burt, the principal retired, Frank, the assistant principal, took over. He wasn't as comfortable having openly gay staff members, nor did he back us up when issues arose.

Eventually, I decided that I had to transfer to another school. After years of renting out the condo I bought when Adam came to live with me full time, I finally had enough equity in it to sell it. I used the money from the sale to further my education. Getting a master's degree would help me get a job at another school. I applied to the Masters in Gifted Education Program at Northeastern Illinois University and was accepted. I started grad school in the fall.

127

# CHAPTER 30

With grad school coming up, I had to cut back on my responsibilities at *Gay Chicago*. It was the perfect time to introduce the writer I'd found to take over my column. Doug Allen was young, seemed to have a good head on his shoulders, and, while his style was different from mine, we worked well together. We wrote the column together for a few months, and in the December 16th column I announced that the end of the year issue would feature my last column. For that final issue, I wrote about writing the column through the years. 1994 would be the first time in more than 15 years that I wasn't writing the gossip column – the most popular feature in the magazine. For that issue, I laid out the After Dark section as I always did. After I went home, Ralph went in and revised my column's layout. As a send-off tribute he included all the pictures that had accompanied my column over the years. Including my many hairstyles!

We took advantage of the change in columnists to make other revisions to the magazine. We renamed the entertainment section from "After Dark" to "Art*i*Facts." Doug Allen's column, now called "Culture Shock," took the place of mine. Our music editor Larry Brewer left and his was a difficult role to fill. As we had expanded our focus from dance music to include Broadway, cabaret and even country. Gregg had contributed one or two book reviews to *Gay Chicago*, so I suggested he take over the music column. He has an encyclopedic knowledge of punk, rock, folk and women's music, all areas our music writers usually avoided. I wanted to make the column less about the latest club hits and broader in scope. Gregg was hesitant, saying he wasn't a journalist. I pointed out that he loved music, and obviously could write, and pushed him to try it for a few months. He grew to enjoy it, and when he realized that it meant record companies would send him demo copies, he was in heaven. Gregg is a collector; books, magazines, and especially CDs, so increasing his collection was a huge incentive. His first feature story appeared in the January 9, 1995 issue.

I'm incredibly proud of my husband. When we met, he was already a successful poet who had published in such distinguished literary publications as *Gargoyle* and *Christopher Street*. He has built a successful career as an entertainment journalist expanding from writing exclusively about books and music to concerts and film. He self-syndicated his work, making contacts throughout the world. At one point, he contributed to more than two dozen publications in the U.S. and Canada and appeared on radio in Chicago. He is one of the most widely read gay journalists, and incredibly well respected. He has conducted one-on-one interviews with such luminaries as Cyndi Lauper, Carly Simon, Tom Ford, Lily Tomlin, and Ang Lee.

## Gregg Shapiro

Gregg Shapiro is one of the leading literary figures in Chicago's gay and lesbian communities and an influential critic of the literary and musical arts.

Locally, his work has been published in *Outlines*, *Nightlines*, *En La Vida*, *BLACKlines*, and *Gay Chicago Magazine*. His music commentaries are heard on LesBiGay Radio.

His reporting on the sexual-minority arts scene is syndicated throughout North America, appearing in Baltimore, Boston, Washington, D.C., New York, West Hollywood, Philadelphia, Miami, Toronto, and Houston.

Shapiro has worked tirelessly to increase awareness of Chicago's gay, lesbian, bisexual, and transgender literary excellence, both within local sexual-minority communities and beyond them. He has been a member of the New Town Writers and the SoPo Writers groups and has organized readings for them. He has supported Gerber/Hart Library through benefit readings and through donations of signed first editions and manuscripts. He has been a participating writer and performer in arts festivals, and adaptations of his works have been produced at Puszh Studios and Bailiwick Repertory theaters.

Though quiet and unassuming, he has received national recognition for his own poetry and fiction. His works were heralded on the cover of *Christopher Street*, the gay literary publication of the 1980s and early 1990s, and some of them have been featured on Dial-A-Poem Chicago. His works have appeared in more than 50 literary journals and in more than half a dozen anthologies.

Shapiro's expertise in popular music is widely recognized. He has been a judge at the Gay and Lesbian American Music Awards for the past three years. He has presented workshops and been on panels at the annual OutWrite conferences. In Chicago, he has taught workshops and judged student work at Columbia College and in the Art Institute of Chicago's Master of Fine Arts writing program. He has also organized group readings and panel discussions at local bookstores.

At every event in which he is involved, Shapiro strives to include representation from all sectors of Chicago's sexual-minority communities. He is one of Chicago's most honored openly gay writers and has long promoted recognition of the city's lesbian, gay, bisexual, and transgender literary and musical talent.

Source: The Chicago LGBT Hall of Fame website at
glhalloffame.org
Shapiro was inducted in 1999

Another addition to the *Gay Chicago* staff was Mark Nagel, who took over the ad sales that were supposed to be handled by Nancy Reiff, who moved on after a few months. Mark joined at the end of '93 and became one of the magazine's most successful ad salespeople. He used his blond good looks and brilliant smile to dazzle many of the bar owners. The magazine was suffering financially, the Internet had killed the phone sex business. After a couple of years of publishing with a full-color glossy cover on expensive paper stock, we returned to a regular newsprint cover.

# Mark Nagel

After joining *Gay Chicago Magazine* in 1993, Mark Nagel quickly realized the power the press played in the advancement of the LGBTQ community. In the years after, his work emphasized the importance of providing a localized publication for Chicago's LGBTQ people, businesses, and causes – both in print and online.

In 2009, after 16 years at *Gay Chicago*, Nagel launched *GRAB Magazine* with Stacy Bridges. Serving Chicagoland and the Midwest, Nagel used this LGBTQ lifestyle and entertainment magazine to also address and educate the community on issues such as HIV and STDs, health, bullying, transgender support, and equal rights.

As a supporter and advocate of numerous LGBTQ organizations and causes, giving back has been important to Nagel. He consistently worked with non-profits in the community, often offering complimentary or discounted advertising. His first response when asked for assistance was often, "How can I help?" The numerous organizations that have benefitted from his assistance include Center on Halsted, Ride for AIDS Chicago, Chicago House, and Heartland Alliance. Nagel's support of Test Positive Aware Network included his personal participation in TPAN's Chicago Takes Off burlesque fundraising event. As co-producer of "The Grabby Awards," Nagel added a philanthropic component to the annual gay adult film awards event, consistently raising tens of thousands of dollars for TPAN. Through various partnerships and fundraising initiatives, he helped raise over $275,000 for various LGBTQ organizations throughout the Midwest.

As a volunteer for the NAMES Project AIDS Memorial Quilt, Nagel helped bring greater awareness of the Quilt to local citizens and aided in the recruitment of volunteers for the National March on Washington. In addition, he served as co-chair of an annual gala that raised essential funds for the organization. Nagel was also an active member of the National Equality Publishers Association, a professional organization for publishers dedicated to the growth, development, and evolution of the LGBTQ media.

Mark Nagel remained steadfast in his dedication to the betterment of Chicago's LGBTQ population and his commitment to serving the community.

Source: The Chicago LGBT Hall of Fame website at
glhalloffame.org
Nagel was inducted in 2017, deceased 2019

# CHAPTER 31

T hings were going well with Gregg. When his lease was up, he moved
the rest of his belongings in. We decided to hold another
commitment ceremony so our family and friends could share in the
joy we'd had at our ceremony at the March on Washington. Though it still
wouldn't be legally binding, it was important to us.

It was also the year of the 25th anniversary of the Stonewall riots. A
massive march in New York City was planned to coincide with the city's annual
Pride celebration, itself a commemoration of the riots, to mark the momentous
events. Gregg and I planned our commitment ceremony and reception for July
3rd, so we decided to attend Stonewall 25 as a honeymoon. So what if the
honeymoon was before the ceremony? We were making up the rules as we went
along!

The Gay Games were being held in New York City that year and timed
to coincide with the Stonewall celebration. While neither Gregg nor I are
interested in sports, we attended the closing ceremony in Yankee Stadium. I
don't know what was more exciting, being surrounded by 40,000 LGBTQ and
allied people in a sports stadium, seeing the 11,000 athletes from 40 countries
parading around the perimeter of the field, or watching performances by gay
icons Cyndi Lauper, Barbara Cook and Patti LaBelle! The following day we

participated in the Stonewall 25 parade, riding on a float with members of the Gay Parents Coalition International.

We returned home and immediately entered the whirlwind of activities for our commitment ceremony. It was to be held later at Gentry, a popular cabaret bar, and one of my favorite hangouts. It was housed in an old mansion off Michigan Avenue and was gorgeous. The main floor featured a large bar area and a cabaret room. The second floor was set up as a restaurant with a bi-level dining room with a white marble fireplace. The restaurant wasn't in operation at the time; but it featured a full bar and a kitchen. I was friendly with the Gentry's owner, Dave Edwards, and had given him lots of coverage at the magazine. He was happy to host our event and offered us the use of the space for free; we just needed to pay for the booze and staff. We hosted about 125 friends and family for a ceremony with a brunch reception following.

Adam flew in from Georgia, where he was stationed with the Marines. My oldest friend Eileen Cooks and best friend Danny Kopelson, completed my side of the wedding party. Gregg's side consisted of his oldest friend Jay Lorden, poet Denise Duhamel and Allison Nichol. We'd asked local cabaret performers (and friends) Beckie Menzie and Don Auxier to perform for the ceremony and provide entertainment at the reception. Don sometimes performed in drag as "Honey West." He asked us whether we wanted Don or Honey to perform. We said we were fine with either.

Don responded, "Well, it will be Honey, she can hit notes Don can't." Honey was, and still is, so beautiful that few people knew she was a man. Don transitioned several years later and now identifies as a woman, adopting her stage name as her legal name. Honey continues to perform and will help out at any benefit or fundraiser when asked. She is a beautiful and warm person that I'm proud to have known for more than 30 years.

I first met Honey when she was performing in a musical in Chicago called *Dirty Dreams of a Clean-Cut Kid*. The show was mediocre, but Honey was fabulous. At that time, she had not yet transitioned and lived and performed under her birth name Don Auxier.

# Honey West

Honey West, 51, for more than 25 years as a cabaret singer and entertainer in Chicago nightclubs and restaurants. She has blended her transgender identity into her career. During that career, she has often performed at benefits for AIDS and other charities. She has also appeared onstage as Honey West and, as Don Auxier, in *Dirty Dreams of a Clean-Cut Kid*, an early AIDS musical.

Transgender entertainer Honey West has been a hit on the cabaret circuit since her debut in the 1990 one-woman show, *A Taste of Honey*. She has won two After Dark Awards as Chicago's Outstanding Cabaret Entertainer as well as several other honors and accolades.

Her charm and versatility as a singer and comedian have attracted a wide and loyal following in Chicago and beyond. She has performed on cruise ships, at awards shows, for dozens of AIDS and LGBT fundraisers, and in numerous concert and cabaret venues from the Park West to Cabaret Metro, and from Gentry to Hotel Allegro. In 1997 she released the CD *Take Honey West Home* and seven years later released a second collection, *My Big Fat Cheesy Lounge Act*.

Among her many gigs, West was seen on Oprah backing up Cyndi Lauper and was crowned Ms. Morton Downey Jr. by a panel of celebrity judges on Downey's talk show. She even performed for Julie Andrews and the company of *Victor/Victoria* at their gala opening-night party. West starred opposite her dear friend Alexandra Billings in the comedy *Vampire Lesbians of Sodom* and has been featured in dozens of stage productions such as *Tony N' Tina's Wedding*, *Pussy on the House*, *Diva Diaries, The Musical*, *Music Kills a Memory*, *The Wizard of A.I.D.S.*, *Sexy Baby*, *Applause*, and *Jerry's Girls*. West also performed as Don Auxier in *Dirty Dreams of a Clean-Cut Kid*, one of the first musicals to address the AIDS epidemic.

She has appeared in the film *Velvets*, which was shown at the Chicago Lesbian & Gay International Film Festival, and recorded the love theme for the Judy Tenuta film *Butch Camp*. In addition, West hosted and was a part of special programming for Amberg Communications and LesBiGay Radio for six years. The popular entertainer has been profiled in the *Chicago Tribune*, the *Chicago Sun-Times*, *Poz*, the *Daily Herald*, the *Boston Herald*, the *New York Native*, Chicago's *Reader*, and other periodicals worldwide.

Throughout her long career, West has worked tirelessly to break down walls and to dispel myths and misconceptions about trans performers. She has enriched the Chicago cabaret, stage, and entertainment worlds and has used her talents to give back to LGBT communities. As co-star Alexandra Billings said, "Honey's never said no to an AIDS benefit and never said no to a charity. She's always been there, free of charge and giving in her spirit and her time."

Source: The Chicago LGBT Hall of Fame website at
glhalloffame.org
West was inducted in 2012

# CHAPTER 32

To keep the commitment ceremony costs down, I catered much of the food myself. We planned a brunch. I bought bagels and made flavored cream cheeses, chopped liver, and salads, all augmented by appetizers from my friend Lauren Verdich, one of the city's top caterers. As I was preparing for our commitment ceremony, I found that few companies were marketing to same-sex events such as ours. I had to make our own groom and groom cake topper, as there weren't any readily available at that time. This, of course, was more than a decade before legally-sanctioned same-sex marriages. If I, who knew so many people in the community, was having a problem finding resources, it had to be nearly impossible for others. At the same time, I noticed that many people I'd known in the '70s and '80s were settling down and having commitment ceremonies or holy unions. And so, I decided to organize a "Gay Wedding Expo." I brought up the idea to my friend Danny Kopelson. We worked on it together, making it a benefit for Horizons Community Services, Chicago's LGBTQ social services agency at the time.

We booked the top floor of Ann Sather restaurant, owned by community activist Tom Tunney. We decided to hold the event the week before Valentine's Day, so we could include romance-based vendors as well as companies specializing in weddings. I bartered free booth spaces to the community's leading florist and caterer in exchange for services I'd use for my own commitment ceremony. I also offered free booths to *Gay Chicago*'s photographer Terry Gaskins as well as all the local LGBTQ religious organizations. Those vendors served as the base for us to build upon. As Danny and I approached potential vendors we first had to explain the concept of a same-sex commitment ceremony, it was so foreign at the time. Eventually we recruited more than 50 vendors. *Gay Chicago* donated ad space and ran a feature story on "A Commitment to Love" the week before the event. Every newspaper in the city, gay and straight, covered the event. We even had television coverage that week! We billed it as "The World's First Gay Wedding Expo" and, to the best of my knowledge, I believe it was.

Now all we had to do was get people there. We had the vendors, but we didn't know how many people would show up. To sweeten the pot, we made admission low (a $2 donation to Horizons) and advertised goodie bags valued at $10,000 (mostly in coupons) for the first 100 people. Of course, that February 6 turned out to be the coldest day of the year, with wind chills of 30° below. We weren't starting until 4:30. I was worried people wouldn't venture out in the cold that late in the day. With the help of Gregg and some friends we set everything up. By the time the vendors started arriving at 2:30, there were already a few people in line. When it came time to open the doors, the line was more than a block long.

Danny and I both have experience producing events, and we had this one planned to the second. Everything went smoothly. The vendors were happy, the event raised thousands for the charity. Danny and I made enough money to take all of our volunteers out for a thank-you dinner, with enough for a weekend getaway for each of us. *Gay Chicago* may have been the first LGBTQ publication to do a "wedding" issue. Ralph was delighted as many of the vendors also took out ads in the magazine when they found out we were doing a feature story on the expo.

## Thomas M. Tunney

In his early 20s, Thomas M. Tunney bought Lake View's venerable Ann Sather Restaurant in 1981, expanded it, and has made it into a virtual community center for lesbian and gay Chicagoans and for older adults.

He has been active in neighborhood business groups, IMPACT, Human Rights Campaign, and the Democratic Party. Besides backing Open Hand Chicago's home-meals program and running a soup kitchen, he has hosted countless gay and lesbian efforts and the White Crane Wellness Center. He has played a unique role in Chicago's gay and lesbian community. At the same time, he has contributed to the betterment of the city as a whole.

Born and reared on Chicago's Southwest Side, Tunney is part of a large family, several of whom have been in the restaurant business also. Tunney earned a bachelor's degree in restaurant management from the University of Illinois and a master's degree in hotel administration from Cornell University. At age 23, he heard that Ann Sather, a Lake View fixture who had opened her homey, Swedish-themed restaurant in 1945, was ready to retire. Sather and Tunney hit it off from the start, and they quickly agreed on a transition that culminated in his buying Ann Sather Restaurant in 1981 and expanding it to its present size.

In the 1980s, Tunney was president and board member of the Lakeview Central Business Association, where he helped to mobilize business owners and bring focus to neighborhood development. He has also served on the board of the North Halsted Retail Merchants Association and was appointed by Mayor Richard M. Daley to the city's Economic Development Commission.

Since 1985, Tunney has served on the board of White Crane Wellness Center, a not-for-profit organization helping older adults to maintain health, dignity, and independence. For three years, Tunney was its president. White Crane has a multi-ethnic dues-paying membership of more than 700 and has made its home at Tunney's restaurant since 1989. Among other results, the relationship has fostered White Crane's involvement in various gay/lesbian and HIV/AIDS issues.

A myriad of other groups have also found a home at the restaurant because of Tunney's support, including Chicago Professional Networking Association, Professionals Over Thirty, ACT-UP Chicago, and Queer Nation Chicago.

After the onset of HIV/AIDS, Tunney provided free meals to hospital patients. He also backed Open Hand Chicago's home-meals program and still consults with the group, besides running a daily soup kitchen for 75 to 100 persons. He has helped the annual "Dining Out for Life" AIDS fundraiser to succeed and has encouraged other businesses to support AIDS Walk Chicago. He is also a business adviser to the late John Baran's Unicorn Foundation, which funds HIV/AIDS- and gay-related causes, and he is a frequent financial donor to gay/lesbian and HIV/AIDS causes.

Politically, too, Tunney has been much involved. He has served on the board of IMPACT and chaired its annual dinner for three years. He is a member of the Human Rights Campaign Fund's Federal Club. He was named as an alternate (Clinton) delegate to the 1992 Democratic National Convention and has actively supported other politicians such as Dawn Clark Netsch, Carol Moseley Braun, Miriam Santos, Richard J. Phelan, and Gerry Studds.

In 1990, Tunney bought and renovated the 909 West Belmont Building, converting it into a vibrant center offering affordable rental to several gay, lesbian, and HIV/AIDS-related organizations. His Hall of Fame induction adds to much other community acclaim he has already received.

Source: The Chicago LGBT Hall of Fame website at
glhalloffame.org
Tunney was inducted in 1995

# Danny Kopelson

Since 1991, he has been an indefatigable arts and AIDS fundraiser and a mainstay of the Chicago Gay Men's Chorus, in which he is a founding member. He has produced special events, including "Dance of Life", that have raised millions of dollars to fight AIDS.

Besides his devotion to Chicago gay choruses, Danny Kopelson has been a tireless fund-raiser on behalf of groups fighting AIDS.

After receiving his 1981 degree from Northwestern University's Medill School of Journalism, Kopelson moved from his hometown of Evanston to Chicago's Lake View neighborhood and immediately became involved in the sexual-minority community.

In his first foray into activism, he was a founding member of the Chicago Gay Men's Chorus, in which he continues to perform after 18 years. He was an early member of the chorus's board and took part in its fundraising and public relations efforts. He was also a founding member of Encore!, a small CGMC ensemble that performed at fundraisers, at other special events, and for HIV/AIDS groups.

Kopelson recently was responsible for raising $25,000 to support the historic "Gay Pride 2000 Concert, Pride at the Pier," which united Windy

City Gay Chorus, Unison: Windy City Lesbian and Gay Singers, and the Chicago Gay Men's Chorus. For four years he was also a member of Windy City Gay Chorus and helped with its fundraising. He has helped to represent Chicago at every conference of the Gay and Lesbian Association of Choruses.

While working for Marshall Field & Company, he took part in its HIV/AIDS outreach efforts and helped raise $1.3 million in 1987 at a Field's-sponsored gala benefit evening. The event, which helped to establish the AIDS Foundation of Chicago and supported the American Foundation for AIDS Research, was the most successful HIV/AIDS fund-raiser in America as of then.

Later, Kopelson handled special events planning, fund-raising, and public relations at the AIDS Foundation of Chicago, producing some of the city's most successful HIV/AIDS events. In only its third year, the AFC gala, "Not Just Song and Dance," raised more than $310,000 as the highest-earning HIV/AIDS fundraiser in Chicago at that time.

Still later, Kopelson joined the staff of STOP AIDS Chicago, where he established the Dining Out for Life benefit and Dance for Life. He is a founding member of Chicago Dancers United, which raises funds for HIV/AIDS work and promotes dance. He took its annual benefits from a net of $20,000 in the first year to $210,000 in the fourth. Still on the group's board and the Dance for Life benefit committee, he co-chaired Dance for Life 2000 and has helped to raise some $1.5 million at its events.

While with Viaticus, a viatical settlement company, Kopelson developed a $250,000 giving program.

Source: The Chicago LGBT Hall of Fame website at
glhalloffame.org
Kopelson was inducted in 2000

# CHAPTER 33

That year, massive changes occurred in Chicago's LGBTQ press. Among them the addition of broadcast media. A small FM radio station, WCBR, leased out time slots to niche markets, mostly foreign language broadcasts. Alan Amberg booked time and began what he called "LesBiGay Radio." He wasn't the first to host an LGBTQ radio program. Two years earlier, Chris DeChant hosted a Sunday night radio talk show in Chicago on WNUA (the smooth jazz station), "Aware: HIV Talk Radio." Amberg's slot was on Sunday mornings from 8-10 a.m. I didn't think he'd be very successful, joking that most of his intended audience would still be sleeping off Saturday night at the clubs. However, he developed a small but loyal following and his audience began to grow.

Amberg brought aboard a variety of co-hosts and on-air personalities, including Gregg as a host, and me paired up with my good friends Marsha Jacobson and, later, Penny Nichol to review restaurants in a segment we called "Partners in Dine." Amberg was so successful in his Sunday morning slot that he eventually moved into the morning drive-time slot, five days a week. Then, later into the coveted evening drive-time slot.

# LesBiGay Radio

Founded by Alan Amberg, for more than 5 years LesBiGay Radio was unique for presenting a Chicago-area broadcast serving a lesbian, gay, bisexual, and transgender audience. It was the nation's first such show in a daily drive-time slot. It launched many service projects, helped publicize the activities of all community sectors, and achieved wide local and national recognition. After years of unique broadcasts on various Chicago radio stations, LesBiGay Radio offered airtime to "every lesbigaytrans voice from all organizations in the Chicago area" and to help bridge gaps among the region's diverse communities.

Launched in June 1994, LesBiGay Radio educated, entertained, and enriched its listeners' lives with information on arts and literature, health, and social service issues. Though there are some 80 gay radio shows in North America, none other has been as comprehensive, convenient, or successful.

It began as a two-hour Sunday-morning show on WCBR, an Arlington Heights, Illinois FM station. Eighteen months later, it moved to WNDZ (750 MHz) for a stronger signal and a daily, morning-commute time slot. The show then aired during the evening drive time from 5 to 7 p.m. Monday through Friday; on WSBC (1240 MHz) by North Side listeners and on WCFJ (1470 MHz) by those on the South Side.

LesBiGay Radio's staff produced 260 shows a year locally, for an average of 10 to 15 hours per week. It offered a mix of general news, traffic, and weather reports; interviews, music, and educational segments; and news of local and national gay and lesbian events. Listeners ranged from Milwaukee, Wisconsin to Bloomington, Illinois, and from Joliet, Illinois to Kalamazoo, Michigan. The show boasted documented listenership in at least 35 of Chicago's zip code areas as well as in other parts of the metropolitan region.

In March 1996, LesBiGay Radio became the first gay business to advertise openly on outdoor billboards in six North Side neighborhoods. It generated hundreds of calls to state legislators on a bill to ban same-sex marriages and sent its own lobbyists to oppose the bill. It produced live broadcasts at Chicago street festivals, offered the first daily gay and lesbian coverage from both major political parties' 1996 national conventions, covered the 1998 World AIDS Conference in Geneva, Switzerland, placed newspaper ads countering anti-gay radical right ads, and ran paid ads for the show itself on general-audience radio and television stations. LesBiGay Radio also sponsored community town-hall meetings and cosponsored numerous local special events. With foundation support, it funded several community empowerment projects, including a series of forums under the name "The Color Triangle: A Different Look at Racism in Our Community." National media coverage often resulted from the show's groundbreaking activities.

In a short period of time, LesBiGay Radio and founder Alan Amberg made national media history while offering Chicagoans a wealth of information and entertainment in an unprecedented format. LesBiGay Radio signed off the airwaves on Friday, April 27, 2001, just one month shy of its 7th anniversary.

Source: The Chicago LGBT Hall of Fame website at
glhalloffame.org
LesBiGay Radio was inducted in 1998

Over at *Windy City Times*, Jeff McCourt had problems with his new staff. In addition to his heavy drinking, he was now also using cocaine. *Windy City Times* was making so much money at the time that the money spent on coke wasn't a problem, but the effects of the drug were. Jeff brought in highly respected Mark Shoofs as editor, but he was soon hired away by mainstream publications. Jeff then hired Louis Weisberg, another highly respected journalist, as the paper's editor. Weisberg brought on another expert reporter, Lisa Neff, and the duo continued Shoof's tradition of top-notch, award-winning writing and reporting. The paper's art director/photographer Jason Smith also won the newspaper many awards. But Jeff's erratic behavior forced Weisberg out too. By the spring of '94, Louis' name had disappeared from the masthead, as had Lisa Neff. Instead, Jeff was listed as editor/publisher and long-time contributor, Dan Perreten, was listed as managing editor. The only award-winning staff member left was Jason Smith, and he soon left as well.

At *Gay Chicago*, I promoted Jeff Rossen to Theater Editor. Although the promotion didn't mean extra money, the title carried a cachet. When I was accepted to grad school, I recommended Jeff replace me as Entertainment Editor. Ralph gave Jeff the job, and I began to step back. It was difficult. Many in the community thought I owned the paper because I was so visible. I stayed on to write my restaurant reviews in a column now called "Place Settings."

Later that fall, Doug Allen, to whom I handed over my gossip column, announced that he was burnt out and would begin writing a different column for *Gay Chicago*. His new column never appeared. Mike Macharello, a local DJ and event promoter, took over the gossip column, now dubbed "Mike at Night."

At the end of September, Ralph and I had one of our few arguments about something I wrote. Ricky's was a diner on the corner of Broadway and Belmont which had long been a popular spot for the LGBTQ community. It was sold, and the new owner changed the name to Nicky's – he was so cheap, he only changed the first letter of the sign. They advertised and requested a review. Many times, when I'm reviewing an advertiser, they are aware that I'm there doing a review. The entire mystique about "anonymous" restaurant reviews is ridiculous. In every big city the identity of reviewers is well known, even those who claim to go in disguise.

Being treated as a guest has never influenced my reviews. I look to see how other customers are being treated, what their food looks like, how quickly their problems are resolved. Sure, the chef or server may give a little more attention to my table, but if they're not good at their job, it will show. I've been treated rudely by staff, made to wait past my reservation time and served awful dishes – even when they knew I was there to do a review.

Nicky's was a case in point. The owner plopped down next to us and insisted we try the cold turkey and fruit plate. He had our server bring over a platter that was placed before us. As he babbled on, we stared down at a plate of dried out turkey breast alongside slices of moldy melon! That was the food we were served when the owner was sitting at our table! The rest of the meal wasn't much better.

My review was pretty brutal, and they pulled their advertising. Ralph was angry with me and we had quite an argument over it. I refused to back down or offer an apology. It didn't matter that I was right and that the restaurant was closed down by the Chicago Board of Health soon afterwards. After that, things began to go downhill for me at *Gay Chicago*. Jeff Rossen, to whom I had turned over the reins, was edging me farther and farther from the center of things. Part of that, I understood; he had to make the entertainment section his domain. I truly would have been happy just writing restaurant reviews. Every time I stopped in the office, my mailbox was empty. Usually, I would get three or four invites a week for special events; restaurants openings, and media dinners. But for several months, there had been very little.

In September of 1995, I did get one invitation sent to my home address. When I showed up, the public relations person handling the event greeted me warmly. Later in the evening, she pulled me aside and asked why I kept sending a writer to events, but never covered them. I explained that I was only writing the dining column now and that Jeff was the magazine's new editor. She looked a bit surprised and then explained that Jeff had been showing up at these events for weeks, but never wrote about them. This put me in an uncomfortable position. Jeff was now my boss, but what he was doing not only undercut me, it made the magazine look bad. I decided to go to Jerry Williams, who handled the business end of things at *Gay Chicago*. I explained what had happened and said I didn't know how to approach Jeff about it. Jerry said he'd take care of it. Later that evening the phone rang, it was Jeff Rossen. I was ready for an uncomfortable conversation, but I didn't expect what happened next. He simply said, "You're fired," and hung up.

The next day I went in to talk to Jerry and Ralph, and they said, "The decision has been made," and they wouldn't discuss it further. I didn't argue or create a scene; I just turned around and walked out. After nearly 14 years, I was no longer a part of the *Gay Chicago* family. I don't know if it was the suddenness of the change or the way it was handled, but I was in shock. I don't remember how I got home, but I remember walking in the door and bursting into tears. I collapsed into a chair, and Gregg took me in his arms. The next issue of *Gay Chicago* came out a few days later. I picked it up and discovered that my name was missing from the masthead. Instead of my "Place Settings" column there was a new column written by Jeff Rossen's friend Tracy Adams.

# CHAPTER 34

I'd been at *Gay Chicago* for 13 years, more than a quarter of my life. I was treated well by Dan and Ralph, and I'd given a lot back. I helped transform it from a bar rag to a legitimate entertainment guide. Winning one of the After Dark Awards I created was a source of pride for theater companies and local actors. Local eateries proudly displayed the Golden Spoon Award I created. Although neither of those awards was created with the intent of spurring ad sales, it did so. I had done so much to make *Gay Chicago* what it was. I had given Jeff a great opportunity. I was hurt and dumbfounded.

I didn't have much time to mourn, as I was in the middle of producing the 3rd annual "A Commitment to Love," this time working with my former roommate and long-time friend, Kelvin Harris. The event had outgrown the space at Ann Sather. In our second year, we'd had to turn away vendors because we just didn't have space for them. Mike Macharello, the new gossip columnist at *Gay Chicago*, had just rented an enormous warehouse near the corner of Halsted and Cornelia. He planned to turn it into a night club, but until he got his liquor license, he was operating it as the Halsted Street Café. Mike appreciated the advice I gave him when he started his column at the magazine and, having the same sense of duty to the community that I did, offered his space.

I knew that one of the reasons "A Commitment to Love" was so successful was the press coverage we'd gotten, not just from *Gay Chicago*, but from *Windy City Times* and Tracy Baim's publications *Nightlines* and *Outlines*. Since Mike was involved in the event, I knew we'd at least get coverage in his column, but without a cover story in *Gay Chicago*, I needed the other publications more than ever.

I dropped into *Windy City Times* and spoke with Jeff McCourt. He steered the conversation away from the wedding expo and into my falling out at *Gay Chicago*. He did it so smoothly, I didn't even realize what he'd done. After pulling out the details of my departure, his first response was that he wanted me to write for him. Although I was tempted, Jeff's erratic behavior made me wary. I got the conversation back to the wedding expo. He agreed to cover it, although he stopped short of offering to be a sponsor – which would have meant free ads. I asked him to let me think about joining WCT and thanked him for his support.

Frankly, I never would have worked for Jeff. Even if I didn't have personal knowledge of his mercurial nature, all I had to do was take note of the revolving door at the editorial office. Jeff McCourt's listing in the masthead regularly changed from editor to publisher to a hyphenated position. Did I really want to add my name to the ever-growing list of those who served as editor? Ray deLaMar, Jen Vanasco, and Kerrie Kennedy followed Tracy Baim, Louis Weisberg, Lisa Neff and Mark Schoofs, not to mention Bill Williams, who stepped in and out of the role so often it was mind-boggling.

The fact that I had a proven track record in the community wouldn't have guaranteed my position. When Jeff started *Windy City Times* he lured another of Chicago's LGBTQ veteran writers, Jon-Henri Damski, to work for him. His column had appeared in *GayLife* and *Gay Chicago*. After Jeff hired Jon Henri, he treated him like royalty, paying him far more than any other columnist, or so Jeff told me numerous times when he was a little tipsy. But Jeff eventually turned on Jon-Henri as well and fired him, for no apparent reason.

# Jon-Henri Damski

Jon Henri-Damski has been referred to as the "gay Studs Terkel."
Born in 1937, he died of melanoma complications in 1997.

He was a columnist for GayLife, Gay Chicago, Windy City Times,
and ultimately Nightlines and Outlines. Damski has penned over 700
articles chronicling gay and lesbian life in Chicago.

Damski kept his finger on the pulse of the community; he knew the
powerful players, as well as the little people. From the playrooms of the
Bijou to the antechambers of City Hall, his colorful neckties and his Cubs
cap were familiar trademarks. Damski captured the sights, the sounds, the
style, and the spirit of the gay and lesbian community.

He also taught adult education, with a focus on current events. A
native of Seattle, Damski earned a Ph.D. at the University of Washington
and later taught Latin and Roman history at Bryn Mawr College.

His lobbying efforts were important to the passage of the Chicago
human rights ordinance in 1989 and the hate crimes ordinance in 1990.

Source: The Chicago LGBT Hall of Fame website at
glhalloffame.org
Damski was inducted in 2004, deceased 1997

No way I was going to jump on the *Windy City Times* merry-go-round.
Plus, it would be a full-time job, and then some. I was still teaching, even if
unhappily. I still had a couple of semesters of grad school left to complete, *and*
my thesis to write. I also wasn't a journalist. I was a features writer and editor. I
didn't have the chops or credentials, and McCourt knew that. He was playing
with me like a cat with a mouse. And we all know what is going to happen to
that mouse eventually!

I left Jeff's office and trudged through the early winter snow and sleet
to the *Outlines/Nightlines* offices on Belmont. I buzzed the bell, announced
myself, and walked up the flight of stairs. I stopped at the reception desk and
could see Tracy in her office directly behind it. I asked to speak to her. She came
out of her office to greet me. That was the first time she actually acknowledged
my existence. I always got the impression that since I wasn't a "hard news"
person, I really didn't matter to her; still, my name carried some weight in the
community. She moved a pile of papers so that I could sit. I assumed she was

aware that I was no longer at *Gay Chicago*, but I didn't know how much she knew. I began by talking about "A Commitment to Love." Tracy immediately offered to be a media sponsor. As we were finishing up and as I was putting on my coat, I casually asked if she'd be interested in my writing for her.

She indicated that I should sit back down. I could tell there was a glimmer in her eye. I think she wanted to snatch me up before Jeff got me. Tracy was notorious for barely paying her writers, if they got anything at all. And to be fair, I also knew she wasn't taking much in the way of salary herself. It was even rumored that Tracy lived in the back of the office. I knew she viewed the paper as a community endeavor and, while I was prepared for less than I made at *Gay Chicago* – which was about $400 a week, not bad for a half-time gig by 1990s standards – I was bowled over by her original offer of $10 a column. Was she living in the 1960s? I wasn't going to be giving my talent away.

We finally negotiated a decent rate – $25 a column. Precisely what I made when I first started at *Gay Chicago* more than a decade earlier. I was to write two columns to run in *Nightlines*; "Eater's Digest" would be a food-related column, alternating reviews, and cooking columns. What Tracy really wanted me for though, was the gossip column. I suggested we call it "Hot Flash," a joke about my approaching middle age. Tracy didn't like that, so we settled on "Hotlines" (I honestly don't know why she had such an obsession with the word lines). I asked if we could start after "A Commitment to Love" was over. I didn't want any of the other publications to pull their support.

The week after the wedding expo, my first columns appeared in *Nightlines*. At the same time, I joined Alan Amberg's Les-Bi-Gay Radio, as an on-air personality, with Tracy's reluctant approval. By then the show had moved to a morning drive-time slot on 750 AM and had a much larger audience. Alan liked to have a balance of male and female on-air personalities. I asked my good friend and fellow teacher, Marsha Jacobson to join me as "Partners in Dine." Since Marsha and I were both teachers, doing the segments from the studio wasn't possible. So once a week, Marsha came to my house before school and we called in and reported from my kitchen, with Marsha on the kitchen phone and I on an early cordless variety. Neither of us had any experience in radio, and Marsha had no performing experience. Marsha is thoughtful and considers what she says before speaking. That's a great attribute in a friend or teacher but leaves a lot of dead airtime on radio. I was used to hosting charitable events and had no trouble keeping up a constant patter, filling in the dead air until she decided to speak. Unfortunately, that came off as my monopolizing the conversation. We eventually came up with a solution by having Marsha write down some comments on index cards before we started the show. After about a month, we fell into a natural rhythm and became one of the show's most popular segments. Eventually the show moved to an evening time slot and that didn't work for Marsha, so Penny Nichols took over as my Partner in Dine.

Looking back, I don't know how I managed to juggle so many disparate parts of my life. I was teaching full-time, attending grad school, writing two columns for *Nightlines*, doing the radio show and, on top of that, I was also working at Sidetrack, helping to produce special events. It was time for the 4th annual "Night of 100 Drag Queens." The event had become one of the most popular fundraisers in the city. I was no longer on the board of the Gay & Lesbian Parents' Coalition International, but I was still a big supporter. That year we were able to donate nearly $5,000 to GLPCI.

As a result of my fundraising and work with Sidetrack, Horizons Community Services asked me to work for them half time in its development department. I gave up the Sidetrack position and moved my efforts over to Horizons, where I had an office and a desk. My official title was "Assistant to the Director of Development." My primary duties were to assist in producing Horizons' "Human First" gala fundraiser, a black-tie affair, and organize smaller events throughout the year. Many of the women on the board were asking for more fundraisers that were women-centric, and a couple of board members wanted more events for Latinas. I thought I'd achieved both when I proposed "Woman Wild," a week of women-centric events timed to coincide with the International Mr. Leather Contest, held over Memorial Day weekend. Since so many events scheduled that week were geared for the male leather community, a bit of counter-programming should have proved successful, and much of it did, but not without headaches.

I booked comedian Kate Clinton for the opening event. Also, several smaller bar parties, concerts and a women's salsa night at Mike Macharello's new nightclub. Kate Clinton's concert was a huge success. It sold out, and the audience, about 80% women, loved it. "Wild Women Week" was off to a great start, but it was all downhill from there. The salsa night event had a total of four people show up, three volunteers and me. The board members who made such a big deal about needing events for Latin women never bothered to show, or even buy a ticket. The remaining events were also poorly attended. The saving grace was the final night's concert, which featured four local lesbian folk singers. Each brought in her own crowd and, though some balked at a $20 ticket, most agreed, once they understood it was a fundraiser for women's programming at Horizons.

I was finishing up grad school, which meant researching and writing my thesis. I knew something had to give and, after the fiasco of "Women's Week," it wasn't a difficult decision. I gave Horizons' executive director, Liz Huesemann, and my boss Paul Fairchild, a month's notice and left after nine months.

# CHAPTER 35

The Chicago Gay and Lesbian Hall of Fame, founded in 1991 to honor persons and entities who have made significant contributions to the quality of life or well-being of the LGBTQ community in Chicago, is the only officially recognized gay and lesbian hall of fame in the United States. It currently has no physical facility but maintains a website, which allows anyone to visit the Hall of Fame at any time. It also has a traveling display, erected in Chicago's main library, the Harold Washington branch, each year during Pride Month and can be installed elsewhere for special events.

The Hall of Fame holds an annual installation ceremony for new members in the categories of individual, organization, or business and "friend of the community" for allies. During the installation ceremony posters honoring the inductees are displayed. The new inductees' posters are then added to the traveling display, and their photos and information are added to the Hall of Fame web site. Chicago Mayor Richard M. Daley attended nearly every installation ceremony each year during his term as mayor. His successor, Rahm Emanuel, has also attended most years since his election. All former individual inductees are invited to review and vote on nominees, whose names are submitted by the community.

# PAPER CUTS

The website and physical displays were once maintained by the City of Chicago's Department of Human Relations. After budget cuts by Mayor Emanuel eliminated that program, the Hall of Fame has been overseen by the Friends of the Chicago LGBTQ of Fame non-profit agency.

I was inducted into the Hall of Fame in 1997, after being nominated three years in a row. I thought I was being intentionally slighted the first two years due to hard feelings over comments I'd made in my gossip column. Now, after having been involved in the process of selecting inductees from a slate of nominees, I know that might not have been the case.

There is usually a bit of in-fighting during the nomination process, with folks lobbying for people they've nominated and, more often, lobbying to keep someone out. We all swear an oath of secrecy, so I can't reveal any specifics. Needless to say, some have violated that oath, telling nominees exactly who said what about them. But I can say that, for the most part, the debate centers on a person's or organization's achievements. Often nominees are rejected because their nomination form was not filled out properly. Sometimes nominees lose out in an attempt by the committee to have a diverse array of inductees. As a white cis-gender man, I was most likely up against many other similar nominees the first few times.

Of course, the year of my induction was the only time Mayor Daley didn't show up to present the award. He had the flu. When I joked that my mother was still waiting for the autographed picture of me with him, he made it up to me by posing for a picture at the next year's induction ceremony.

It was a great honor to be chosen. I was especially happy to have my husband Gregg, my mother, my sister, Donna, and Adam witness the induction. You'll notice that my father wasn't listed among those attending. He couldn't be bothered. I was not disappointed, as I had long ago written him off. He pulled the same thing the opening night of my first musical, *Spin Cycle*. My mother dragged him to the show, but he left during intermission and went to get a hot dog. He actually said that to me, as if it were a viable excuse for missing the debut of his son's first musical. My father passed away a few months past his 86th birthday. At the time of his death he still couldn't understand why I wouldn't speak to him.

# CHAPTER 36

As the '90s drew to a close, Chicago's LGBTQ publishing world went through a major upheaval. Jeff McCourt's drug and alcohol problems reached new heights. His behavior became even more erratic. After making a big deal about hiring Jon-Henri Damski, he fired him just as abruptly. Staff members came and went so quickly that sometimes their names never even appeared in the masthead.

When Damski died a year or so later, *Outlines*, for which Damski was writing at the time of his death, ran a two-page spread on his career. Jeff ran a front-page story in *Windy City Times*, singing Damski's praises. In the article, written by then editor, Louis Weisberg, there was no mention that McCourt had fired Damski. That irked more than a few people, including a long-time supporter of McCourt, Albert "Bill" Williams. At that time Williams was a senior writer at the highly respected alternative weekly, the *Reader*. He filled in as editor at *Windy City Times* from time to time when Jeff fired whoever was serving in that position at the time.

Williams wrote a letter to the editor that was a condemnation of McCourt. Williams addressed the letter to McCourt, but of course, he copied it to both *Gay Chicago* and *Outlines*. Both ran it. The letter which appeared in the November 27, 1997 edition of *Gay Chicago* called out McCourt for his "graceless attempt to promote (and perhaps redeem) himself by being quoted in praise of the writer he abruptly and unfairly fired last year. What deluded arrogance."

Jeff weathered that storm and things quieted down for a bit. The community was relieved that the pace of the AIDS crisis was slowing somewhat. The discovery of a new drug combination, called a "cocktail" was beginning to save and prolong lives. By the spring of 1998, for the first time in a decade, there were issues of the local papers without obituaries. The economy was improving, and we brought "Commitment to Love" back to Ann Sather and attendance rebounded. That June, the Pride issues of the newspapers were massive. *Windy City Times* made history by being the first LGBTQ newspaper to exceed 200 pages, with dozens of full-page ads from major retailers and corporations. Jeff McCourt may have been mercurial, but he could market a newspaper.

Even *Gay Chicago* set a record for itself, publishing an issue with 150 pages. *Outlines*, never as good at marketing as the other papers, published a 48-page issue. A new player emerged that week; *Pride*, which had appeared sporadically in the past, put out a large-format magazine with glossy four-color pages throughout. David Cohen, the editor/publisher offered a publication that was little more than an ad book. *Pride* made it through a year of quarterly publications and then would appear sporadically for a few years.

About the only publication that wasn't thriving was *Gab*. The pocket-sized magazine, one of the few LGBTQ publications in Chicago for which I had never written, was published sporadically from 1994-1995. *Gab* sprung from another alternative magazine, *Thing,* which was founded and published by Robert Ford, a Creative Director of Rose Records and a frequent contributor to local music publications. *Thing* was one of the first successful 'zines, but only produced ten issues. Ford and some of his contributors went on to *Babble/Gag/Gab* – the name changed after a series of lawsuits. The 'zine had a punk aesthetic. Its contributors mostly used pseudonyms (Astro Boy, Miss Margie, Fire Chick, Hi-Fi Bangalore, etc.). It did have a few legit writers among its contributors; including music lists by DJ Freddie Bain, straight gender-bending activist Lindsey Cochran, and a newsy column by Richard Cooke. In lieu of a masthead was the line: "Babble is a Malone design, published by Propago Publications." It took pride in making fun of community leaders (including me), often in a mean-spirited way. Like many under-funded alternative publications, it faded away after in-fighting and personality clashes.

## The Publisher and the Porn Star

Jeff McCourt's behavior could be erratic, but nothing prepared those who knew him for his obsession with the porn star, Ryan Idol. We all knew that Jeff appreciated muscular young men. Ryan Idol, a one-time *Playgirl* centerfold, whose real name was Marc Anthony Donais, claimed to be straight and, indeed had a girlfriend. However, he was, as they say, "gay for pay." He'd appeared in several gay porn movies and was trying to parlay that fame into a legitimate acting career by starring in a play for Bailiwick Repertory's annual Pride Series. McCourt was smitten upon meeting the handsome porn actor and spent a great deal of money on drugs and romancing Donais. In a 2007 article in *Chicago* magazine by Robert Sharoff, the author quotes Donais, "He was somebody I'll never forget. He was really like a best friend, a big brother. He would have me in his office all the time to show off and stuff. And he would be wielding his power, and I identified with that."

In Sharoff's article, Louis Weisberg, editor of *Windy City Times* at the time, recalls it differently, "We'd have editorial meetings where Jeff would be sitting there with white powder around his nose, drinking booze out of a bottle with Ryan Idol asleep on the couch. At some point, we just knew this wasn't going to work – that this was no way to run a business."

Steve Alter, a *Windy City Times* staff writer at the time, added, "In some kind of fucked-up way, they cared about each other. They were two highly narcissistic, very on-the-edge types of personalities who were using each other for image, for money, for drugs, for sex. In spite of all that – and I know how strange this sounds – I think there was something real there."

McCourt's obsession with Idol even led him to bankroll a production to promote the porn star's "legitimate" acting career, which became the talk of the LGBTQ press nationwide. The syndicated columnist Billy Masters, who usually traded in Hollywood gossip, even mentioned the situation in his "Gotcha!" column that ran in LGBTQ papers across the United States In the column Masters wrote, "Could it be that a certain porn actor is bringing his own kiss of death to the publisher of a certain gay rag? So say friends of both men who tell me that the publisher is obsessed with this thespian and has been filtering mucho dinero to the impoverished former porn idol. The outcome?

The publication suffered a mass exodus of staff members and the porn actor returned to Southern California – as all porn stars do eventually (along with the swallows). That's life in the Windy City."

Donais finally parted ways with McCourt when someone with even deeper pockets took an interest. Donais eventually appeared in a number of plays, most of which showcased his nude body. In 1998, Donais was seriously injured after a drug-induced fall from a third-story New York City apartment window. In 2012 Donais was sentenced to 12 years in prison for attempting to murder an estranged girlfriend.

———————

Eventually, McCourt's objectionable behavior proved too much for a number of *Windy City Times* staffers and they walked out. It was déjà vu. This group of staffers learned from Tracy Baim's example and found financial backing for a new publication. The walkout was timed for maximum effect. They disappeared the day before the deadline for the Market Days issue of the newspaper, the biggest issue of the year other than Pride. They took the stories they were working on with them. By that time, McCourt had destroyed so many relationships that few were willing to step in and help him.

Community activist, and one-time McCourt confidant, Rick Garcia, told *Chicago* magazine, "It was like watching a train wreck. You had someone with enormous gifts and talents who contributed to his profession and community in ways that were unparalleled but who was spinning out of control."

*Windy City Times* editor Louis Weisberg, associate editor Lisa Neff and photographer and art director Jason Smith left to form *Chicago Free Press*, taking with them Bill Feld as general manager and Mark Olley as advertising manager. The financial backing came from insurance magnate Jerry Matusik. *Chicago Free Press* immediately set itself apart from *Windy City Times* by rejecting the privileged insider status McCourt had created and listed itself as "A common voice for a diverse community." It was also one of the first LGBTQ publications to include an Internet presence in its initial vision.

Jeff McCourt immediately went on the offensive and released a press statement claiming that, "Reports of *Windy City Times*' demise are greatly exaggerated. I will continue to publish the *Windy City Times* to the best of my ability and with the same commitment to quality and service to the community, this week, next week and for the foreseeable future, just as I have for the past 15 years." As an indication of his increasingly unstable mental state, he added, "I believe that the departures were part of a carefully orchestrated plan to devalue, if not destroy, this publication."

Jeff struggled along for a few years, essentially publishing, editing, and writing the paper on his own, but he never fully recovered. From then on *Windy City Times* never was the same. As all of this played out, I was glad I hadn't let Jeff hire me after I was fired from *Gay Chicago* – by this time I was no longer an insider, I was removed from the fray.

I was handing in my food column for *Outlines,* but I stopped writing the gossip column while in grad school and no longer missed whatever cache it gave me. I was increasingly satisfied with my teaching career at my new school, where I was appreciated and encouraged. Although I had stepped back, I was happy to see Gregg blossoming as an entertainment journalist. He'd gone from writing a weekly music column at *Gay Chicago*, and then in *Nightlines* to covering books, theater and film, and compiling the entertainment calendar.

By October, Gregg was named Music and Theater Editor for *Outlines.* He had also begun self-syndicating his work with his reviews and celebrity interviews running in more than a dozen LGBTQ publications across North America. As a capper on a great year, I'd nominated Gregg for induction into the Gay and Lesbian Hall of Fame. He got in the first time. I guess he hadn't made as many enemies as I had!

# CHAPTER 37

One evening I got a phone call from Steve Roath, an actor who had appeared in *Spin Cycle*, my first play. After my experiences with Frank DePaul, I'd sworn off theater, limiting my output to writing shows for my students to perform for school-wide assemblies. The most ambitious I got was a 30-minute musical adaptation of the children's book, *Ira Sleep Over*. So, I was a little surprised by the call from Steve. He'd just moved back to Chicago and started his own theater company and wanted to do a 20th anniversary revival of *Spin Cycle*. I was glad to hear from him, but had to tell him, that I didn't have any copies of the script or score, as they'd been lost in one of my many moves. He'd saved his copy of the script and score so that problem was solved. I gave him my blessing – by this time Frank DePaul had died from AIDS, so his permission wasn't required.

With *Musical*, the script that Frank had pirated from me, I was not allowed to make changes. In turn, I felt Frank's changes had hurt the show. So, with *Spin Cycle*, I asked Steve to first consult with me about any changes. The few suggestions Steve made improved the script. Also, the cast was stronger than in the original production. In fact, it was a superior production in every way.

However, the show was dated. In the age of *Will & Grace* it wasn't ground-breaking or daring. Looking back, it should have been done as a period piece. I invited the staff from my new school to attend a production, and many of them did, some more than once. Seeing a play I'd written performed live on stage was a hell of a way to introduce myself to a bunch of new co-workers. Some of them were in awe and predicted that I'd be going to Broadway or Hollywood soon. It was sweet, but I had no delusions about that. The show did decent, not great, box office, during its run. The best thing was that I got a video of the production and a copy of the script.

It also got my creative juices flowing again. Throughout my life I've occasionally awoken in the middle of the night with some concept buzzing in my head. Sometimes it's an idea for a lesson, or a project around the house. Once I woke up obsessed with putting together the family trees for the characters on the television show, *Friends*. I've learned that if I don't get up and make some notes, I'll never be able to get back to sleep. This is a symptom of my manic-depression, I suppose, but, it's one I'm willing to live with.

One night I woke up with a story and some very vivid characters in my head. I went to the computer and started writing my notes. The first thing I did was write character descriptions, then an outline of the story. I was still writing when Gregg got up in the morning. When he stopped by a little later to ask if I was going to take a break soon, I waved him off. When he came by later, I waved him off again, a bit angrily. That's when he pointed out to me that I'd been writing for 12 hours non-stop. I'd just begun my first novel.

Technically, it wasn't my first, I had written the two serialized stories that ran in *Gay Chicago*, but this was the first thing I had written like this in years. When I went to stand up from being hunched in front of the computer, I ached, but I felt wonderful. I hadn't realized how much dealing with the toxic situation at my old school had drained my creativity. I had the first draft of the novel, *Show Biz Kids*, finished in two weeks. Of course, it would go through many revisions. However, the basic story about the children of stars who become stars themselves remained.

Feeling the freedom from the tyranny at my former school let me see that I was experiencing it, to a lesser degree, with Tracy. Her refusal to pay a reasonable fee for my work was unacceptable. She was still paying me $25 a column. Even for reviews set up by a PR company, I would still have to leave a tip and pay for parking, so I was often making no money at all. It had been more than three years and I knew that she obtained a number of restaurant advertisers because of my column, so I thought it was time for a raise. Tracy refused. Rather than argue, I just turned, walked out the door and went directly to the offices of the *Chicago Free Press*, precisely I had done years before at *Gay Chicago*.

I introduced myself and asked to speak to the editor. Lisa Neff and Louis Weisberg led me to the conference room. I left a few minutes later with an offer for twice the pay and the title Food Editor. I got home and gave Tracy two weeks' notice; my last column appeared in *Outlines* in the Memorial Day issue. That happened to be the week of my last on-air appearance on Les-Bi-Gay Radio. The next week *Chicago Free Press* ran an article announcing that I was joining their staff.

By the spring of 2000, *Windy City Times* was struggling. Not only had McCourt lost his key staff, but he had also alienated almost everyone he knew. Years of drug and alcohol abuse had taken its toll on McCourt. At some point along the way, he became HIV positive, although he wouldn't admit it. The few times we would meet, I could all too easily see the signs; the facial wasting and the weakness. He was sick and broke. After struggling for almost a year, he sold *Windy City Times* to Tracy Baim. She had coveted the name for years. Although it wasn't anywhere as influential and respected as it had been in its heyday, the title still had a cache. Tracy struck a deal, snapping it up for $250,000. She immediately re-branded *Outlines* as *Windy City Times*, while keeping *Nightlines* as a bar and club guide.

After selling the paper, Jeff McCourt slipped into the shadows. As HIV decimated his body, he spent more time in Northwestern Memorial Hospital than he did out of it. When he was at home, his paid caretaker was his only companion. Soon dementia set it. He spent the last months of his life in a Gold Coast nursing home tended to by a companion hired by his family.

The man who changed the world of gay publishing would be largely forgotten by an entirely new generation of the LGBTQ community.

# CHAPTER 38

C hicago now had two strong newspapers, *Chicago Free Press* and *Windy City Times*. *Gay Chicago* was still the primary source of entertainment news for the LGBTQ community. I was content to write my restaurant reviews, cooking columns and occasional travel features for *Chicago Free Press*. I also started to pick up gigs with on-line guides, especially the *Chicago Tribune's* Metromix. More and more folks were looking to the Internet for reviews and it appeared that it might be a renaissance for LGBTQ journalism. All three publications created on-line versions, but they were little more than digital copies of the print publications. That year also saw the debut of Chicago's first completely on-line LGBTQ "magazine," GoPrideChicago. None of the newspapers and magazines considered the website a serious contender, but it chugged along. Since overhead was minimal, the site was able to maintain a presence and grow slowly.

In the meantime, I continued with my community involvement. We held "Night of 100 Drag Queens – 9" – we started numbering them arbitrarily at some point. By now, the event had become one of the city's best known and most successful fundraisers. The show expanded to two nights to accommodate the demand for tickets and it became a fundraiser or Equality Illinois. Liquor companies vied to be sponsors and Sidetrack had two special stages built and brought in professional lighting and video. By this time, I did little more than help audition the acts and manage the performers backstage. So, I give credit to Chuck Hyde, Art Johnston and Pepe Pena from Sidetrack. I was no longer involved, except as a "special guest" now and then.

No sooner had we swept up the glitter from Night of 100 Drag Queens and Halloween than I was back at Sidetrack preparing for another event. My friend Danny Kopelson and I and Sidetrack produced an Oscar party as a benefit for the Chicago Gay Men's Chorus. When I was done with that benefit, I began working with the Lesbian Community Cancer Project on its annual Valentine's Day "Coming Out Against Cancer" gala. My friend Jessica Halem, the agency's executive director, roped me into coordinating the event's silent auction. She knew that there's nothing more effective than an anal-retentive queen with a spreadsheet. I'm proud to announce that the two years I chaired the silent auction, it raised the most money. Of course, it helped that we auctioned off a guitar donated by Melissa Etheridge and Ellen Degeneres' "Swan" dress from the Emmy Awards.

As Tracy Baim took over *Windy City Times*, she began rebuilding the ad revenue and the status of the paper. At *Gay Chicago*, Ralph Paul's health deteriorated. After his life-partner Michael William's death, he was never the same. Jerry Williams, who Ralph brought on as co-publisher, began to handle more of the business end of the magazine. It was later discovered that Jerry was embezzling funds. Rather than press charges, Ralph let him go without fanfare in October of 2001. Stacy Bridges, who had joined *Gay Chicago* a few months earlier as an ad rep, was named his replacement. Within a year, Bridges would be listed in the masthead as the magazine's general manager.

Changes were also taking place earlier that year at LesBiGay Radio. Alan Amberg was battling with his board of directors as they tried to reduce his on-air presence. It was finally reported in the January 11, 2001 edition of *Gay Chicago* that he signed over LesBiGay Radio to the Bonneville Chicago Radio Group, a subsidiary of the Mormon Church. By the end of the year, Baim expanded her Windy City Media Group to include Windy City Radio. An ad in the December 12 edition of *Windy City Times* touted the broadcasts on "WCKG 105.9 Sunday, 10:30-midnight." Tracy later changed *Nightlines* to *Nightspots* magazine, getting over her fixation with the word "Lines" once and for all. She named St Sukie de la Croix as editor and Woody Bryant as head of ad sales.

At *Chicago Free Press*, Jerry Matusik was finding the entire business too stressful. He sold the publication to lawyer David Costanzo and moved to West Hollywood, where he later died from cancer. Costanzo was very involved with the paper's finances, and had many plans, none of which he followed through on. He spoke with me about bringing back the "Commitment to Love" wedding expo. By this time, the Netherlands had passed gay marriage, and people were talking about it in the U.S. – it became legal in Massachusetts two years later. Costanzo wanted to make it a huge event at a downtown hotel. I agreed to participate, but only if it were a benefit for Equality Illinois. Costanzo agreed, but he lost interest before we got to the initial planning stages. I did get him to donate free ads as he promised. However, the event, renamed the Heartland Wedding Expo, was not what we hoped, and it made little money for Equality Illinois. By then mainstream wedding expos were courting the same-sex wedding market, and they had the resources, infrastructure, staff, and experience to overshadow our little show.

Costanzo also decided to go after the bar and club guide market that *Gay Chicago Magazine* and *Nightspots* already covered. He assigned Kerrie Kennedy to head up the *GO Guide*, a publication geared to the LGBTQ club scene. Costanzo was surprised when it wasn't immediately successful. After several issues with insufficient advertising, he altered the focus to a "lifestyles" publication with each issue focusing on one topic; health, fitness, fashion, etc. He kept publishing it, even though each month the racks were still filled with the previous issue when the new issue came out. The distributors would dump dozens of copies in the trash to make room for the current issue.

At *Chicago Free Press*, Costanzo exhibited erratic behavior not seen since the days of Jeff McCourt at his most tweaked out. David would show up at the offices in the middle of the night to hunt the rats that plagued the place. If he caught one, he would nail it to the wall. He would show up infrequently during the day, but when he did, it was usually with a young man in tow. Weisberg, Neff, Smith and the rest of the staff were at their wits' end. They thought they had left that behavior behind them.

As a contributor, I spent little time in the offices, just dropping in to check my mailbox and pick up my check. Or, more often, to bring back a check that bounced. But even I was able to see the deterioration. As a reward for my patience, Louis Weisberg assigned me to an all-expense-paid press junket to

France. This was not long after 9-11, and the whole anti-France sentiment was hurting tourism in the country. The French Tourism Bureau decided to focus on gay tourists who would be least likely to side with the Republican anti-France crusade. They invited about a dozen journalists from the LBGTQ press across the country for a week-long tour of the Loire Valley and Paris. One of the journalists spoke a bit of French, and whenever he spoke the locals complimented him on his accent. At the end of the tour, he told me that the entire week he had been imitating the Warner Brothers cartoon character, Pepe LePew. Those of us who spoke less French still had a great time. We were wined and dined, and all went home to write glowing reviews. After the articles ran in various publications around the country, gay tourism in France skyrocketed.

# CHAPTER 39

By 2003 Gregg had been promoted to "Senior Entertainment Writer" at *Windy City Times*. Of course, Tracy being Tracy, that didn't mean any more money, she would often give people titles rather than raises. One person who was able to play Baim at her own game was St Sukie de la Croix, he managed to get the titles and a pittance more money from her. Gregg had no such luck with her, though. She was incredibly abusive to him, would yell at him and demean him. He begged me to get him a gig at *Chicago Free Press*. Both Lisa and Louis wanted to hire him, but they had to wait until it was financially feasible. Finally, he made his debut in the 2005 Pride issue. We were at the same publication again.

St Sukie de la Croix moved to Chicago from Bath, England, in 1991 and made an impression in Chicago LGBTQ community immediately. No one in Chicago had ever met someone like him. I doubt there is anyone in the world anything like him. It was easy to spot him in his goth/punk attire. When I first met him, I wrote him off as just another poseur, but then began to see there was more there than I expected. First was his acerbic wit, his tongue should be registered as a lethal weapon. He then began writing for Tracy's various publications, providing a fresh take on Chicago's LGBTQ community.

# St Sukie de la Croix

St Sukie de la Croix, 60, for his 25 years as a social commentator and researcher on Chicago's LGBT history. He has published oral-history interviews; lectured; conducted historical tours; documented LGBT life through columns, photographs, humor features, and fiction; and written the book *Chicago Whispers* (University of Wisconsin Press, 2012) on local LGBT history.

St Sukie de la Croix, the man the *Chicago Sun-Times* described as "the gay Studs Terkel," came to Chicago from his native Bath, England, in 1991 and in the years since has painstakingly explored, documented, and revealed the queer lives and history of his adopted home.

His interviews, columns, and archival tidbits have given depth and colorful substance to the LGBT history of Chicago, often by chronicling and exploring the underground, bar-life, and nightlife aspects of the LGBT communities. He has had regular columns in local publications or online news and entertainment sources such as *Chicago Free Press, Gay Chicago, Nightlines/Nightspots, Outlines, BLACKlines, Windy City Times*, and *GoPride.com* as well as numerous others outside the city. His popular blog Bitter Old Queen focused on history and humor and was published on the *Chicago Tribune* Media Group's website *Chicago Now*. In addition, he has contributed to publications such as PerVersions: The International Journal of Gay and Lesbian Studies.

In 2008 he was a local historical consultant as well as an on-screen interviewee for the WTTW television documentary Out & Proud in Chicago. In 2005 and 2006 he had two of his plays, *A White Light in God's Choir* and *Two Weeks in a Bus Shelter with an Iguana*, performed by Chicago's Irreverence Dance & Theatre company. From 1998 to 2000 he scripted and conducted the Chicago Lesbian and Gay Tour for Chicago Neighborhood Tours, a division of Chicago's municipal tourism authority. The tours were characterized by de la Croix's historical expertise as well as his signature humor and wit.

In addition, de la Croix has served on the board of directors of Gerber/Hart Library and Archives and in 2009 was on the programming committee of Reeling 28: The Chicago Lesbian & Gay International Film Festival. A popular and engaging lecturer, he has spoken at an array of venues from Chubb Insurance to Boeing and from Horizons Gay Youth Services to a Chicago Area Gay and Lesbian Chamber of Commerce awards ceremony.

His crowning achievement came in 2012 when the University of Wisconsin published his in-depth, vibrant record of lesbian, gay, bisexual, and transgender Chicagoans, *Chicago Whispers: A History of LGBT Chicago Before Stonewall.* With a foreword by the noted historian John D'Emilio, the book received glowing reviews and cemented de la Croix's deserved position as a top-ranking historian and leader in preserving the rich past of LGBT life in the Windy City.

Source: The Chicago LGBT Hall of Fame website at
glhalloffame.org
de la Croix was inducted in 2012

St Sukie de la Croix and Gregg Shapiro worked together at several of Tracy Baim's publications, then later at *Chicago Free Press, ChicagoPride.com,* and *Gay Chicago* and developed a close friendship. They have toured together promoting their books. We've spent many Christmas Eves together before we retired to Florida and St Sukie and his husband Ian to Palm Springs, California. The miles apart haven't dampened Sukie's and Gregg's friendship, they speak to each other almost daily.

In the summer of 2005, Gregg and I produced the Outmusic Awards. For years the event took place in New York City. Dan Martin and Michael Biello, composers and songwriters who founded the awards to recognize outstanding achievements by openly LGBTQ musicians, needed a break. We offered to take over the event for one year, if we could produce it in Chicago. It was quite the undertaking, but we managed to pull it off, with a few friends helping us out.

The Chicago Cultural Center donated the space for the opening reception and the awards presentation. The W Hotel put up our marquee-name presenters, awardees and hosts, including actor/singer Lea Delaria, actor/singer Randy Jones (the cowboy from the Village People), and musician June Millington (who led the early women's rock group, Fanny). Everything went smoothly. Well not everything. I'd been warned that Lea was a diva, and initial negotiations with her manager filled me with dread. When I picked her up at the airport, she was as friendly as could be, her only request, that we stop for ribs as she hadn't had lunch.

Throughout the weekend she was a delight to work with, although she did have a bit of a melt-down when the hotel lost the script for the awards ceremony, and it wasn't ready for her at rehearsal. Luckily, I had printed up an extra copy and handed it to her. She was all smiles again and was the least demanding person I dealt with that weekend. Producing the event was great fun and allowed me to meet some legendary performers. Still, we were happy to hand the event back to folks in New York the following year.

By the middle of 2005, I had a final draft of my novel *Show Biz Kids* ready to go and submitted it to a number of publishers. I had no delusions that it was great literature. In promoting the book my standard line was, "Some writers want to be the next Faulkner or Steinbeck, I want to be the next Jacqueline Susann." I did think that the book had the makings of a best-seller – don't all authors – at least within the LGBTQ community. It followed the format popularized by Susann, and later by Jackie Collins.

The various characters were loosely based on real people. There was a Liza Minnelli-esque character; another was loosely based upon Candice Bergen and a pair similar to Jane and Peter Fonda, among others. Their stories interwove and incorporated historical figures and events from the early 1950s through the 1970s, culminating in an attempt to blow up the Statue of Liberty in 1976. It was campy and outrageous.

I sent inquiry letters, along with a couple of sample chapters to 100 publishing houses and got 99 rejection letters. I expected it to be snapped up immediately. After all, everything else I had written worked out that way. I was in for a rude awakening. It was a check on my ego. I did get a letter from the editor at one publishing house asking for the full manuscript. I packed it up and sent it off expecting to get a contract. Instead, I got a mean-spirited, nasty rejection. If the editor disliked the novel that much, he must not have liked the sample pages he had already read, so why request the entire manuscript?

Impatient, I decided instead to go to a self-imprint (aka a vanity press). It cost a couple thousand dollars, but I got hundreds of copies and had a product to push. I did readings at bookstores all over town. I knew that gay best-selling author E. Lynn Harris had started the same way. Traveling around and selling his novels out of the trunk of his car until he was discovered. I thought I'd do the same. However, I didn't have the determination or drive Harris had – and maybe not the talent – and the books languished. I sold about 400 copies and still have a case of books in the back of the closet. Perhaps if I had heard of the numerous rejections J.K. Rowling got for her Harry Potter series before it was finally picked up, I might have pushed a little harder, but then again maybe not. I just don't have the fortitude to keep pushing for something, no matter how much I believe in it. Perhaps I've been spoiled by the instant gratification I got for my first attempts at writing a column and then later a musical. I'm fairly certain that if Sarah and Steve had passed on my column or someone wasn't willing to produce *Spin Cycle*, they too would have been set aside.

Although I was happy in my teaching position, the first decade of the 21st century had its share of trials and disappointments. Ralph Paul Gernhardt died in June of 2006 nearly 30 years after founding *Gay Chicago News*. When I found out about Ralph's death I burst into tears, he truly was like a father to me. I went to the *Gay Chicago* offices, now located on the ground floor of the same parking garage it had been in when I worked there. I didn't know what else to do. I walked in and the first person I saw was Karen Ross, the same face I saw when I first stepped into the offices in the 1970s. We just sat and held hands for a minute, then she said, "We need a drink."

Over drinks, we shared stories about a man who had changed both of our lives. A few weeks later, *Gay Chicago* put out its 30th-anniversary issue, and it was a loving tribute to Ralph Paul. He may not have had the business savvy of Jeff McCourt, but he had a big heart. He never turned away a charity event ad or a request for a donation. If Jeff McCourt was the brains of Chicago LGBTQ press, Ralph Paul Gernhardt was its heart, Dan Di Leo was its libido, and Tracy Baim was its determination.

That July, Gregg was going to Montreal to cover the Jazzfest. He usually runs away from jazz, but it was a press junket held in conjunction with the Out Games. We both went as guests of the Montreal Tourism Board. Two years later, in 2008, we were guests of the New Orleans Tourism Board in conjunction with the "Saints and Sinners" literary festival. The tour consisted of meals at the city's best restaurants mingled with tours of historical sites. Writing for the LGBTQ press may not pay well, but occasionally the perks make it worthwhile.

# CHAPTER 40

Queen Elizabeth described 1992 as her annus horribilis; mine was 2007. There's nothing worse for a parent than seeing your child suffer and being unable to do anything about it. My son Adam wandered around after his discharge from the Marines. He lived in California for a while. By that time, we had healed the rift in our relationship. He returned to Chicago and we became close.

Adam became a county sheriff, a job he loved. The irony wasn't lost on me; an old hippie like me with a police officer for a kid. I never let him play with guns when he was young, and here he was carrying one for his job. However, he seemed happy, so I was glad for him. When he turned 30, Adam gained weight and within a few years, he was obese. One Friday night, I got a call from his girlfriend, Erica. He was in the hospital. He had collapsed at work but was resting comfortably. Gregg's family's annual picnic was the following day, so we said we'd stop by the hospital in the afternoon after the picnic. As we were driving to the hospital the next day my phone rang. It was Adam's doctor asking me why I wasn't at the hospital. That's when I learned how serious his condition was. His doctor told me he might die that day. We raced to the hospital to find Adam was unconscious. Adam's body had stopped processing fat and it entered his blood stream. They were draining the blood from his body, removing the fat from the blood, then re-administering the blood back into him. Seventy percent of his pancreas was necrotic and had to be removed. The procedure that required him to be put into a drug-induced coma for weeks as the pancreas was shaved away little by little.

Erica and I alternated sitting with him. She was a nurse and switched to nights, so she could stay with him during the day. I went to the hospital after school every day, so she could go home and sleep for a while before heading back to work. There was a time there when we didn't think he was going to make it. I sat next to him and applied lotion to his hands and feet, stroked his hair, and talked to him, not knowing if he heard me or not. He was in the hospital for ten months, most of that in the ICU. It took another full year before he returned to work.

He was now down to a manageable weight, but it didn't change his bad habits. It didn't take long for him to start smoking again, and he also started to gain weight, which meant he was eating badly. Within a year he collapsed at work and was in the hospital again, this time for almost two months. It took a third bout to make him realize what he was doing. He lost most of his thirties to this illness and he still is undergoing surgeries.

I look at photos of me from before Adam got sick, compared to now, and I look 30 years older. Some of that is time, but a lot of it is stress. Eventually, Adam came to his senses and started following a healthier lifestyle. He'll never be entirely back to what he was, but he manages to get through every day and I'm grateful for each of them.

# CHAPTER 41

F ed up with David Costanzo's antics, Weisberg and Neff left *Chicago Free Press*. For a short time, they were replaced by Gary Barlow, a former reporter for the paper. Matt Simonette, another reporter, was then listed as interim editor before taking over as editor-in-chief in October of 2008. At *Windy City Times*, long-time contributor Andrew Davis was editor.

Simonette seemed to be stabilizing things at *Chicago Free Press*. In February of 2009, the newspaper debuted a new logo, layout, and design. Later that month, we brought back the Golden Spoon Awards, which I launched at *Gay Chicago* years before. Simonette followed through by sending certificates to the restaurants that had been included and made the announcement of the awards the cover story of the February 26 issue.

That summer David Cohen rebranded his irregularly produced publication, *Pride*, as *Pink*, which eventually morphed into *The Pink Pages*, a listing of LGBTQ businesses. Craig Gernhardt, Ralph's son, had worked on and off at *Gay Chicago* over the years. After Ralph's death, he stepped in thinking he would take over. The only problem was that Craig didn't have the skill set or personality to do so. He clashed with staff, advertisers, and readers. Realizing his shortcomings, he brought in Michael Harrington to serve as publisher. Harrington was an odd choice. Although he had served as editor of the Chicago Teachers' Union newsletter, he had little experience in journalism. He also had his share of controversy. He had been president of the board of directors of the Frank M. Rodde Fund, set up to fund a gay and lesbian community center. Harrington resigned from the board under a cloud of suspicion after the fund bought a building, which was then sold in a "sweetheart" deal, leaving the fund nearly depleted. His tenure at *Gay Chicago* was short-lived. He lasted only a couple of months before Craig asked him to leave and brought in the magazine's former production manager, Bert Glidewell listed as publisher. He didn't even last as long at Harrington. Within a week, Craig Gernhardt had fired him, and the magazine had no publisher listed in the masthead.

Matt Simonette had his hands full at *Chicago Free Press*. David Costanzo continued to behave erratically, would often show up at the office with his two ill-behaved dogs terrorizing the staff. Those of us working for the paper were told to "hold onto our checks for a few days" before depositing them. Even when we did so, the checks bounced. In December of 2009, in a highly publicized protest, the majority of the staff and contributors walked out. The *Reader*, *Chicago Tribune* and *Sun Times*, all reported the departure of key staff. David and his advertising and business managers, Jeff McBride and Bill Feld went into damage control.

A week later, on December 23, the *Reader* reported, "Editor in chief Matt Simonette, art director Vincent Lane, and senior writer Amy Wooten had walked out, and several freelance contributors were leaving with them. But Costanzo said he and general managers Jeff McBride and Bill Feld have been contacting those contributors, and everyone they've reached has agreed to stick with the paper."

I was among those who were contacted by McBride and Feld. I was offered the position of Food and Travel Editor if I returned, and Gregg was promised Entertainment Editor. Although the positions didn't mean an increase in pay, it was a bump in stature. I asked for a meeting with David Costanzo. At the meeting, I said that I would come back only if everyone was paid what they were owed, even those who weren't returning. David promised to do so. In the first issue of 2010, on January 7, Kerrie Kennedy was listed as the editor, but I wasn't listed in the masthead at all, nor did my column run.

The next issue, dated January 14, featured a new logo, and the masthead only listed two columnists; Paul Varnell and Jennifer Vanasco. That issue was only 24 pages. The following week I was still not in the masthead, although my column ran. I called Kerrie and reminded her of the promise David made to me. She informed me that I would be listed in the next issue as Food/Travel Editor. When the next issue hit the streets, I was again not listed, although my column ran. In a second call to Kerrie, she claimed that I was never promised the editorial title.

As soon as I hung up on Kerrie, I called Mike Macharello, who wrote the gossip column after I left *Gay Chicago*. Mike owned Circuit nightclub and had started a magazine geared to the club scene. The magazine, called *boi*, had little in the way of content. Mike had been after me for a while to come aboard as editor. Frankly, the focus of the magazine held little interest to me. I was too old for the club scene and had no desire to go to clubs and cover appearances by second and third-tier recording artists. Macharello promised me that he wanted to expand the scope of the magazine to become a "lifestyle" publication. His current editor was moving out of town and Mike was willing to give me complete creative control. Things weren't working out at *Chicago Free Press*, so I agreed.

I asked to hold off starting for a few weeks, since Gregg was still writing for *Chicago Free Press* and was listed as an editor in the masthead, as promised. I didn't want to make things difficult for him. I simply wasn't going to send in a column anymore. Although I was no longer submitting articles to *Chicago Free Press,* my name was finally listed in the masthead.

The first edition of *boi* with me as editor was the St. Patrick's Day issue. When the March 18 issue of *Chicago Free Press* came out, my name was still on the masthead. I don't know if they thought I might come back, or just didn't bother to update the masthead. Things at *Chicago Free Press* were in freefall. The next issue, my name was gone.

Contrary to what he had promised, Costanzo went back to his old ways and erratic behavior. On May 3, 2010, Kerrie Kennedy sent out a press release announcing that *Chicago Free Press* was ceasing publication, "Due to health problems, publisher David Costanzo is no longer funding the operation of *Chicago Free Press.*" Consequently, the paper's April 29 issue was not published, and it is not expected that any additional issues will be published."

I brought Gregg over to *boi* to write a music column and got Michael Elder, a personal trainer, to write a fitness column. Michael had appeared in the revival of *Spin Cycle*. He was a good singer and dancer and cute as a button, but I didn't expect much in the way of writing talent. He surprised me by being quite good. We didn't have much of a budget, so I offered Michael free ads for his business as a personal trainer in exchange for his column. Other than Michael and Gregg, I wrote all of the articles. Much as I had at *Gay Chicago*, I used pseudonyms for various articles, most of them puns; fashion articles were by Anita Taylor, the auto section was by Parker Kerr. Before I brought Michel Elder aboard, I even wrote fitness articles under the name Illya Kostalis, the name of a muscle in the lower back. Mike Macharello said he was getting good feedback on the improved content of the magazine and we continued to grow. We even became the official guides for Pridefest, Midsommarfest, International Mr. Leather, and Mr. International Rubber.

Meanwhile, Craig Gernhardt saw the problems at *Chicago Free Press* as an opportunity. Gary Barlow had already left *Chicago Free Press* and had been working for *Gay Chicago* for a few months. Craig hired editor Matt Simonette and Amy Wooten, the senior writer for *CFP*. Craig sent out press releases making the announcement. The *Reader* picked up the story, written by none other than former *GayLife* and *Windy City Times* editor, Albert Williams. The story led with the following: "The recent upheaval at the LGBT newsweekly *Chicago Free Press* has inspired *Gay Chicago Magazine* to introduce a new feature, '*Gay Chicago* Newswatch,' by former *Free Press* news editor Gary Barlow. The 'Newswatch' column debuts in the December 31 issue, hitting the streets and the web today. And then next month, says *GC* owner Craig Gernhardt, 'I'm bringing Amy Wooten aboard to help cover political races.' Wooten, former senior writer at *Free Press*, was one of several editorial staffers to walk out at the *Free Press* earlier this month."

# CHAPTER 42

T he new incarnation of *Gay Chicago* wasn't very effective; *Windy City Times* was too well established, and advertising dollars weren't as plentiful as they were in the past. That didn't stop Craig from announcing new additions to the staff in May of 2010, most of which were former entertainment writers. He hired back Jeff Rossen and Gregg as well as St Sukie de la Croix – formerly with *Windy City Times*. Craig seemed to be making inroads. In an attempt to appear successful, he put out a Pride edition of 106 pages. Craig had previously lost Mark Nagle, his top ad salesman, who left with Stacy Bridges to form their own entertainment magazine, *Grab*. To pad the issue, he practically gave away ads for free. In an attempt to save money, he moved the magazine's offices to the basement of the Abbott Hotel, long known as a fleabag populated by drug-dealers and hookers. That move did little to burnish *Gay Chicago*'s already tattered image. Craig tried to spin it as part of the new life of the magazine and held a small party celebrating the January 4, 2011 issue, *Gay Chicago* 35<sup>th</sup> anniversary.

Craig's "reinvention" of *Gay Chicago* as a newspaper didn't last. He couldn't sell enough ads to pay his writers, and he battled with everyone he brought in as a publisher. In a last-ditch attempt, he created a not-for-profit, the *Gay Chicago* Foundation for LGBTQ Education and Research, which he hoped would publish the magazine. He brought in another co-publisher, Dane

Tidwell, who promised big changes and an influx of capital. It never happened, and after a few issues it was announced that *Gay Chicago* was going to be a completely online publication. The last print copy was in November of 2011. Craig and Dane even convinced me to come back and write restaurant and food news, hoping he'd get restaurant advertisers. Mike had no problem with me doing so, as long as I remained at *boi*. I wrote one column and submitted it, but the magazine folded before it even ran. Matt Simonette moved on to *Windy City Times*, other writers either moved out of town or on to other projects and professions.

As the year progressed, I saw a lot of my former colleagues passing away. Ron Helizon, affectionately known as "the Polish Princess" died in March. Near the close of 2011, Paul Varnell passed away, leaving me as the sole writer from the early days still being published regularly. There were still a few people around who wrote for the papers at one time or another: Bill Kelley, Rex Wockner, Marie Kuda. But none of them were still writing in Chicago's LGBTQ press on a regular basis. Bill Kelley and Marie Kuda have since passed away. Wockner, whose work has appeared in more than 325 gay publications in 38 countries, now mostly writes for his own blog.

The once-thriving LGBTQ press in Chicago was now limited to four publications; *Windy City Times*, the only legitimate LGBTQ newspaper, and three publications covering bars and clubs; *Nightspots*, *boi*, and *Grab*. The ChicagoPride website grew steadily, and now has editions in Washington D.C. and LA, as well as Chicago. As it celebrated its 10th anniversary, the site announced it would be featuring three new writers; St Sukie de la Croix, Gregg Shapiro, and me. Since *boi* was bi-weekly, I was able to cover more restaurant reviews and dining out news on the ChicagoPride website.

I continued writing for ChicagoPride and editing *boi* magazine for a number of years. In 2012 I retired from teaching. Gregg and I began to spend the winters in Wilton Manors, Florida, a town with a heavily LGBTQ population adjacent to Fort Lauderdale. Before we would leave for the winter months, I would stockpile a dozen or so reviews for ChicagoPride. I brought my computer from *boi* down to Florida with me and, thanks to the wonders of technology, was able to sync my computer with Mike Macharello's, which contained the layouts of each issue. I continued editing and writing for *boi* for another year or so.

After a few years, Gregg and I decided to move to Florida permanently. I had to give up writing for *ChicagoPride*. Gregg continued with them for several of years before he was dropped in a series of cut-backs. I continued editing *boi* for a few years, until it too began to lose advertisers. Mike Macharello couldn't afford to pay me or any other writers and now produces the magazine on his own. Eventually, he moved to an online-only format.

As I write this, *Grab* and *Windy City Times* have continued to thrive.

---

I stopped writing for Chicago publications in 2016. I've been lucky enough to write for several publications in South Florida. I started writing travel pieces for *Florida Agenda* and its bar guide companion *Guy Magazine*. After a few too many bounced checks from *Florida Agenda/Guy*, I walked into the offices of the competing *South Florida Gay News*, just as I had with *Gay Chicago* and *Chicago Free Press*. I approached editor Jason Parsley and publisher Norm Kent about writing a dining column. I was hired and am now the Food and Travel editor for that publication and a contributor to its quarterly lifestyle magazine, *The Mirror*.

Gregg was also writing for the *Florida Agenda* and *Guy Magazine* until they went under. He was approached immediately by *The Miami Herald* to contribute to its new niche magazine *Palette*. I also got writing assignments for that publication for a while before it too went under. Gregg now contributes movie reviews to *SFGN*'s website and writes for a monthly Fort Lauderdale-based publication/website *OutClique,* as well as his self-syndicated work in newspapers and magazines around the U.S. Gregg has also carved out a successful career as a poet and author and has had 10 books featuring his poetry and short stories published. I occasionally pick up gigs from nationally based web publications, such as *Out Traveler,* and work with the local theater company, Island City Stage, working with its youth outreach program.

It's been a wild ride; I met people and went to places I never expected to go in my wildest dreams. And it's all because I said "Yes" when someone asked me, "Do you think you could do it?"

# ACKNOWLEDGEMENTS

I don't throw around this word lightly, but I've been truly blessed by having some wonderful people in my life, many of whom are directly, or indirectly responsible for my being able to live such a rich life and have the experiences that led to this book. First to the two most important men in my life; my extraordinary and supportive husband Gregg, who suggested I write this book, and my son Adam, who's been there through all of it. I love you both more than you can imagine. To my publishers St Sukie de la Croix and Ian Henzel for shepherding this project along and for the generous use of your home and archives. To Dan Layman and Robin Alexander for reading early drafts and providing feedback. To my wonderful sisters Donna and Diane, thanks for kicking me in the pants when I needed it. To my extended family of in-laws, who have shown what a family can be. To Danny Kopelson, the Ethel to my Lucy (or vice versa). To "The Group" for more than 50 years of friendship. Finally, to the fur babies who have enriched my life over the years; Sasha, Dusty, k.d. and Coco.